AN INVITATION TO

PEACE & REST

IN A WORLD OF STRAIN & STRESS

BRIAN DOLLEMAN

Requests for information should go to
brian@northwestleader.com

Published in Seattle, Washington.

Edited by Angela Hagebusch, Doreen Dolleman, & Kristin Loehrmann

Printed in the United States of America

ISBN: 1503114945
ISBN-13: 978-1503114944

DEDICATION

This book is dedicated to my Ashy (Ashah Joy Elizabeth Dolleman). Your persistence in asking, "Daddy, are you going to dedicate your book to me?" has paid off. You win. And you make me smile.

CONTENTS

INTRODUCTION

Life with God is easier than we think. Most of us are simply trying too hard. We're straining and we're stressing, but all that effort is for nothing.

God doesn't want your works, He wants you.

And there's more.

The life that He has for you includes peace and rest.

Sounds too easy, doesn't it? Just too good to be true.

Exactly.

Too good to be true is God's specialty.

Unmerited. Undeserved. Unexpected.

The impossible.

That's His way.

He is the true Hero of the story—the Hero who saves the day, settles the score, makes a way where there seems to be no way...

He loves us more than we know.

He loves us now, today. And not just some future, perfected version of ourselves, but our real selves. He's not disappointed in us. Actually, He delights in us.

I'm pretty sure all the really important things He wants us to know in life, He whispers to us. I hope you will hear God whispering as you read this book.

The pages that follow are some things I've heard Him whispering to me lately.

Yeah, yeah, I'm up at Brooklyn, now I'm down in Tribeca right next to De Niro, but I'll be hood forever.
—Jay-Z (Empire State of Mind)

I'm giving you an unshakable peace. Yes, you live and work in hostile territory—but there isn't one good reason to be concerned. I am victorious over it all.
—Jesus (John 16.33 paraphrased)

1. BROOKLYN

Several years ago I led a team of college students on a trip to Brooklyn, NY to work with underprivileged children. Of course we were excited about all the typical New York sights and landmarks...

Ground Zero
Central Park
The Statue of Liberty
Grand Central Terminal
The Empire State Building
The Brooklyn Bridge
Rockefeller Center
Times Square
Canal Street
Wall Street
Tribeca
Macy's

Honestly, I also had shopping on my mind—this is New York we're talking about (and this was before we had H&M, All Saints, or Zara in Seattle). But our purpose wasn't tourism or shopping. Several times I reminded our team, "We've come to roll up our sleeves and serve." The reminder coming out of my mouth was just as much for me as the team of students I was leading.

YOGI BEAR

We were partnering with Metro Ministries, famous for what they call "Yogi Bear Sunday School," an outreach to kids in the Brooklyn area. Started in 1980 by Bill Wilson, the ministry reaches over 20,000 kids in New York City each week. That's 20,000 kids from some of the toughest neighborhoods anywhere.

After a red-eye flight from Seattle to New York, our team checked in and had a brief introduction to Metro Ministries. Our tour guide was a Puerto Rican, twenty-something staff member nicknamed "Scar" because of the obvious scar on the right side of his face. Scar had our clear and undivided attention.

We were given Yogi Bear T-shirts and Metro Ministries lanyards with instructions to wear them because "People in the 'hood love Yogi Bear Sunday School and won't shoot you if they see you're with Yogi Bear." I wanted to ask if he was wearing his Yogi Bear T-shirt when he obtained his scar, but decided to hold the question for now.

Yikes! I wasn't in the habit of wearing cartoon character clothing, but it looked like this would become my new favorite T-shirt, at least while I was in the Brooklyn 'hood.

I was beginning to think this ghetto was a little more intense than the South Seattle neighborhood of Skyway that I grew up in. I always said I grew up in the 'hood, but now that seemed like a ridiculous over-statement.

SOUNDS IN THE NIGHT

On our first night with Metro Ministries, we bunked down in their gym. The guys slept on one side of the court, the girls on the other. Sleeping on a concrete gym floor is uncomfortable, but there were a few other unsettling details, like team members hearing "rustling" noises under the bleachers. Rumors of rats began spreading like "news" on TMZ.

We had a student with us who had severe attention deficit hyperactivity disorder and would often do rather strange things. After midnight on our first night there, he plugged in a vending machine that lit up the entire gym with its fluorescent glow. We all started complaining. Next, we heard the clinking of quarters into the machine. He selected Mountain Dew, and the can of pop came crashing down. He popped the top and started drinking. We were concerned about how much noise this guy would be making through the night with him all hopped up on caffeine and sugar, but he unplugged the vending machine, threw away his empty can, laid down, and promptly fell asleep. Thank God for minor miracles.

We certainly weren't used to the sounds of the ghetto through the night...

We heard some intense yelling that sounded like it could be on the Maury Show right outside our door at 1:30 in the morning. By the way, I didn't tell you about the door. The double metal gym doors were padlocked with a huge chain from the outside to keep us "safe." I kept wondering what the fire escape plan was.

A car alarm went through that annoying sampling of alarm options 28 times before the owner finally turned it off. Ten minutes later the alarm was going again. Some of our guys memorized the alarm pattern and mimicked it later in the night.

Loud firecrackers exploded in rapid succession—or maybe it was gun shots being fired. The gym didn't have any windows, so we couldn't look and see what was happening.

And there was the music of an ice cream truck driving through the neighborhood slowly at 3:00 AM. Uh, yeah that was strange.

The following day, after our wonderfully refreshing night's sleep in Brooklyn, I asked one of the Metro Ministries staff members about the whole ice cream truck thing. Were people really buying Creamsicles at that hour? Or maybe the ice cream truck driver had gotten really high and lost his sense of night and day? What's the story?

I wasn't expecting his answer: "No, but sometimes the trucks also sell cigarettes and maybe even drugs—so if you hear the music in the middle of the night, it's not for ice cream."

Ice cream trucks that sell drugs? Wow.

We were in a strange and unsettling place. It was like a war zone. We were living and working in hostile territory.

And although I continued to be surprised with every piece of new information about this foreign place, I wasn't worried about the safety of our team. It was weird. Maybe it was the Yogi Bear T-shirt that brought me a sense of peace...

or maybe it was something else entirely.

INTRODUCTION & CHAPTER 1 BIG IDEAS

Life with God is easier than we think. Most of us are simply trying too hard. We're straining and we're stressing, but all that effort is for nothing.

God doesn't want your works, He wants you.

And there's more; the life that He has for you includes peace and rest.

He loves us more than we know.

All the really important things He wants us to know in life He whispers to us.

Even while in strange and unsettling places, or when we live and work in hostile territory, there is a deeper peace that comes from God.

"I'm giving you an unshakable peace. Yes, you live and work in hostile territory—but there isn't one good reason to be concerned. I am victorious over it all." (John 16.33 paraphrased)

QUESTIONS
FOR INDIVIDUAL &/OR GROUP STUDY

1. What strange and unsettling places have you been before?

2. Can travelling outside your comfort zone be good for you? How?

3. How have you been stretched / what have you learned when you put yourself in a new environment where everything is different from what you are used to?

4. Have you ever felt like you were living and working in hostile territory? Explain.

5. What "Yogi Bear T-shirt" safety-net have you been given to protect you while living and working in hostile territory?

6. Have you experienced a deeper peace even while being in a strange and unsettling place or while living and working in hostile territory? Where did that deeper peace come from?

BROOKLYN

Yo, we at war. We at war with terrorism, racism, and most of all, we at war with ourselves.
—Kanye West (Jesus Walks)

Tears on the mausoleum floor, blood stains the coliseum doors...
—Jay-Z (No Church in the Wild)

If you act like wild animals, hurting and harming each other, then watch out, or you will completely destroy one another.
—Paul (Galatians 5.15 GNT)

2. ESCALATION

We have a problem.

We don't do peace very well.

It seems like our default position, our normal, is stress. Like the David Bowie and Queen song says, we are "Under Pressure."

American culture is and has always been bloody. There is constantly another war we're fighting. We are violent, aggressive, and we love a good revenge story.

We have a John Wayne image of Jesus. We want Him to be tough and leathery, good with a gun, after all the bad guys, the last man standing. But Jesus doesn't sound one bit like this...

I won't be wronged, I won't be insulted, and I won't be laid a hand on.
(The Shootist, 1976)

Young fella, if you're looking for trouble, I'll accommodate ya.
(True Grit, 1969)

Out here a man settles his own problems.

(The Man Who Shot Liberty Valance, 1962)

Out here, due process is a bullet!
(The Green Berets, 1968)

Don't say it's a fine morning or I'll shoot ya.
(McLintock, 1963)

Don't apologize, it's a sign of weakness.
(She Wore a Yellow Ribbon, 1949)

Now you understand. Anything goes wrong, anything at all... your fault, my fault, nobody's fault... it doesn't matter... I'm gonna blow your head off. It's as simple as that.
(Big Jake, 1971)

It makes us feel all warm and fuzzy on the inside to see our Jesus as a John Wayne character, with a "my gun is bigger than yours" and "the law is on my side" world view.

But is the Kingdom of God anything like a John Wayne movie?

Before you answer that question, take a moment to consider the teaching known as the Beatitudes (Matthew 5.3-12). Here, Jesus says the meek will inherit the earth and the peacemakers will be called the children of God.

Of course, John Wayne isn't making movies anymore. And we don't use horses for transportation or carry six-shooters around on our hips...

But maybe we're still living out "Cowboys vs. Indians" in the modern world.

THROWING DOWN AT THE SHOPPING MALL

Do you know where the expression "road rage" originated? I'll give you a hint: it's not from China or Norway or Spain. If you guessed it came from the United States of America, you're right.

We are the kings of escalation.

We fight...
We fight for our pride. We fight for our place.
We fight to protect. We fight to advance.
We fight for ourselves and for our kind.

And something always happens in the process: we exchange peace for whatever it is we've been fighting for.

Without peace, we live on edge. This life on the edge causes us to be frazzled, frayed, full of tension and angst.

To put it plainly, we have a problem.

I recently witnessed multiple shouting matches and near-fights at the shopping mall in my community. One of the verbal fights was between pedestrians and the driver of a car looking for a parking spot.

It's almost as if people are quoting lines from a John Wayne movie to one another:

I won't be wronged, I won't be insulted, and I won't be laid a hand on.

Young fella, if you're looking for trouble, I'll accommodate ya.

Out here, due process is a bullet.

And all this because someone cut in line, took your parking spot, looked at you the wrong way...

Talk about first-world problems! Going to the shopping mall is gravy—it's extra, it's all bonus, a privilege. I mean, really, it's a leisure activity. Unless you're there as a thief or you work at Auntie Anne's making pretzels, it typically means you have time and money to spare. There are hundreds of thousands of items to choose from at the mall. It even has a "food court" – with more options and calories than anyone could ever need. Most of our malls have movie theaters in them too. See what I'm saying? Leisure activity.

Something about all the stress and angst at the shopping mall struck me as odd. I kept thinking, shouldn't we be walking in with smiles on our faces? Why all the tension and aggression?

And if that's what we act like when life is good, how do we behave when things are really challenging? We have a problem!

ANIMALS AND THEIR PEOPLE

Of course, we're not all "throwing down" in mall parking lots. Some of us like to hold it in, but that doesn't mean we have a greater sense of peace and rest in our lives.

I'm by nature reserved and quiet; it takes me a long time to think about what I want to say. This makes me a terrible trash talker (and by terrible I mean I'm no good at it). Sure, I will think of something great to say, but it's always hours or even days too late. The only person who ever hears my great comebacks is me.

I used to do this when I worked at the animal hospital. As bad as cat scratches and dog bites are, the real danger came from their owners. Dealing with the people was always a greater challenge than dealing with their pets. People would be rude, insulting, and at times would even threaten us.

One time an angry client yelled "B----, I'll rock your world!" at another customer in the lobby because she called him a cruel pet owner. That was weird. Is that even an expression people use? I'll rock your world? In fact, doesn't it usually mean something good, like "I will make you amazed" or "this will blow your socks off" or something like that?

Anyway, they kept yelling and threatening each other all the way out to the parking lot, so I called the cops. While the people were having an altercation, their pets stood by calmly. Just another day at the veterinary hospital in Rainier Beach where the pets are fine and the people are out of control.

When someone would say something way out of line, I never had a response. I would always just take it, quietly, with sort of a non-expression on my face. My wheels would be spinning. In that moment, I'd be thinking, "Did they really just say that? Am I the only one here who thinks this is crazy? Who talks like this? What's going on? Is this a dream? I can't believe this is happening right now." Nothing would come out of my mouth, not because I didn't want to argue or fight or hurl insults back at them, but because I couldn't think of anything good to say in time.

Then, for the rest of my day, I'd be replaying what they said over and over in my mind. I'd think about it, get mad about it, and work on coming up with some good lines that I should have said (and believe me, I would come up with some doozies). In my mind, the situation that was over and done with hours ago would be escalating. I would actually get more upset after the fact than I was in the moment. Crazy, I know.

The thing is, some of us are trash-talkers in the moment, and some of us are talking trash in our heads hours after the moment. Either way, we're on edge.

With all the straining and stressing, we're under constant pressure.

It's a problem.

Especially for those of us who call ourselves Christians.

Why?

Because the way of the Kingdom is not strain and stress.

Jesus, the Prince of Peace, gives us something different. What He gives is counter-cultural. It's subversive. No "Out here, due process is a bullet" lines from Jesus. This doesn't look or sound like anything we're used to hearing or seeing in our culture.

"I am leaving you with a gift—peace of mind and heart. And the peace I give is a gift the world cannot give. So don't be troubled or afraid." (John 14.47 NLT)

Jesus isn't just giving us a Yogi Bear T-shirt and lanyard to keep people in the neighborhood from shooting or stabbing us. He's giving us something greater...

Peace.

This peace is internal. It's a treasure contained deep within ourselves. It doesn't shrink like a cotton T-shirt that has been laundered too many times. It doesn't fade or fray, or get lost, or donated to the Goodwill.

It is ours to have and to keep. It is God's gift to us.

The way of the Kingdom is not strain and stress.

Instead, God wants us to have peace and rest.

CHAPTER 2 BIG IDEAS

The way of the Kingdom is not strain and stress.

"I am leaving you with a gift—peace of mind and heart. And the peace I give is a gift the world cannot give. So don't be troubled or afraid." (John 14.47 NLT)

Jesus isn't just giving us a Yogi Bear T-shirt and lanyard to keep people in the neighborhood from shooting or stabbing us. He's giving us something greater...

Peace.

This peace is internal. It's a treasure contained deep within ourselves. It doesn't shrink like a cotton T-shirt that has been laundered too many times. It doesn't fade or fray, or get lost, or donated to the Goodwill.

It is ours to have and to keep. It is God's gift to us.

QUESTIONS
FOR INDIVIDUAL &/OR GROUP STUDY

1. How have you seen escalation at work in our culture?

2. Why do you think we are more used to living on edge than a life of peace?

3. Do you tend to be a trash talker in the moment or do you internalize the hypothetical dialog? Do you wish you could do the other?

4. How is God's way of peace counter-cultural?

5. Why do you think most Christians today don't really accept Jesus' teaching in the Beatitudes as a way of life?

6. How is internal peace greater than an external safety net?

White knuckle ride, I'm on it.
It's not so easy to control, pressure.
It's not so easy to control, pressure. There's no easy way to make it better.
—Jamiroquai (White Knuckle Ride)

Then wolves will live in peace with lambs, and leopards will lie down to rest with goats. Calves, lions, and young bulls will eat together, and a little child will lead them.
—Isaiah (Isaiah 11.6 NCV)

3. KNUCKLES

I'm not much of a thrill-seeker; I'm no adrenaline junkie. In fact, there are more theme park rides that I won't go on than I will. I have rules for this: no rides that go upside down, no spinning, and no motion simulators. Basically, if the ride goes fast and in a straight line, I'm in.

I think my daughter has inherited my boring sensibilities.

Recently, while at Disneyland, we went on the Indiana Jones ride. She was white-knuckled the whole way. When we got off the ride, I asked her, "Did you like the ride?"

Ashah said, "No! I had my head down and eyes closed the whole time. And then when I finally did open my eyes, it was the worst part—that big boulder thing was rolling toward us."

What a funny way to experience a theme park ride – head down, eyes closed, white knuckles. I think we sometimes go through life that way too.

WHEN A GANGSTER WALKS BY

While on the Brooklyn ministry trip, I was assigned to visit a neighborhood in the projects. These towering buildings with hundreds of low-income, government subsidized apartments were clustered around a park. Our job was to visit the kids from these buildings who participate in Yogi Bear Sunday School.

These projects were heartbreaking and you could sense the hopelessness there. The buildings and surroundings were dark, cold, and impersonal. There were no flowers blooming, no welcome mats at the doors. Instead, there were bars on the windows and gang sign graffiti on the walls.

Violence and crime are the way of life there. And we were there to love the kids growing up in this grim reality.

The Metro Ministries staff member I came with had a "divide and conquer" game plan. She would do visits in half the buildings, and I would do the other half. She assigned Damien, a ten year-old boy who lived in those projects, to help me out.

Damien was quiet and somewhat timid, but helpful. He knew the kids in the buildings. With Damien's help, we made it to all the apartments and visited with all the families on our list. We even finished our visits before the Metro Ministries staff member completed hers, so we waited in the park for about thirty minutes.

While sitting on a bench in the park, we talked about life: basketball, food, school, church, family, and rap music. As we chatted, Damien suddenly stopped and froze. His face became pale, body tense, and he looked noticeably shaken. Damien's hands gripped the bench and his knuckles were white. He seemed to be paralyzed with fear. Something was wrong.

He whispered, "Don't say anything. Just look down. That guy walking towards us is a gang member. His gang shot and killed someone last week. I'm scared."

My only guide to this New York City war zone was a frightened ten year-old boy. I trusted he knew what he was talking about. He obviously wasn't exaggerating or playing tricks on me. He was genuinely frightened, and I could see Damien was hoping to ride through this storm unharmed.

It's funny how moments like these, although only a matter of seconds or minutes, can seem like they last forever. Damien, in his paralyzed state, was my mentor—and I followed his example. I looked down. I didn't speak or move.

Time passed ever so slowly.

Nothing happened.

With the gang member now completely out of sight, we breathed and relaxed and spoke again. We had survived the storm.

Before long, the Metro Ministries staff member arrived, and we were off to our next adventure in Brooklyn.

LOOK UP AND SMILE

I'll never know how much of a threat that gang member really was to us. Would he even bother people like us? Did he care about the bald man and ten year-old kid sitting on the park bench in Brooklyn? Did we have any reason to fear? Were the white knuckles necessary?

I really don't know. We both had our Yogi Bear T-shirts and lanyards on. I tend to think it would've been fine to just look up and smile at the approaching gang member.

In fact, that's my plan: the next time I run across a gang member who was recently involved in some sort of a shooting or stabbing, I'm going to look up and smile. Really. Why not?

You see, I don't want to live paralyzed with fear.

I'm still not going to choose theme park rides that spin, go upside down, or are the motion simulator types, because I don't consider throwing up a way to have a good time...

But I don't want to go through life with my head down, eyes closed, all white-knuckled.

I know I can't control the outcome, but I can choose to live as a lamb at peace among the wolves. If I get eaten, so be it. But until that happens, my plan is to look up and smile.

After all, Jesus promised peace and told us not to live in fear...

"Peace is what I'm giving; peace from me to you. This is not something the world has to offer. So don't live paralyzed with fear; there's no need for white-knuckles with me." (John 14.27 paraphrased)

I'm convinced God does not want us to go through life with our heads down and eyes closed for the entire ride. It's time to look up, smile, and enjoy the ride!

CHAPTER 3 BIG IDEAS

"Then wolves will live in peace with lambs, and leopards will lie down to rest with goats. Calves, lions, and young bulls will eat together, and a little child will lead them." (Isaiah 11.6 NCV)

I don't want to live paralyzed with fear.

I know I can't control the outcome, but I can choose to live as a lamb at peace among the wolves. If I get eaten, so be it. But until that happens, my plan is to look up and smile.

After all, Jesus promised peace and told us not to live in fear...

"Peace is what I'm giving; peace from me to you. This is not something the world has to offer. So don't live paralyzed with fear; there's no need for white-knuckles with me." (John 14.27 paraphrased)

I'm convinced God does not want us to go through life with our heads down and eyes closed for the entire ride. It's time to look up, smile, and enjoy the ride!

QUESTIONS
FOR INDIVIDUAL &/OR GROUP STUDY

1. What's the worst theme park ride you've ever been on? Why was it so terrible?

2. Do you have "rules" for theme park rides? Which ones will you not go on? Why?

3. What was a white-knuckle experience you recently had?

4. Have you ever been paralyzed with fear, only to realize later that response wasn't necessary? What does that tell you?

5. Why is "looking up and smiling" so difficult at times?

6. What does choosing to live as "a lamb at peace with the wolves" look like?

I'm a tortured soul, I live in disguise.
Rest in peace to the leader of the Jackson 5.
 —Jay-Z (Welcome to the Jungle)

Those who follow godly paths will rest in peace when they die.
—Isaiah (Isaiah 57.2 NLT)

4. R.I.P.

I'm not gonna lie, I've got issues.

Recently in a sermon, I said, "Yeah, I'm a man of faith and I'm a piece of work. How ya like that?" Funny, the people did like it. Quite a few of them clapped. Maybe it was just confirming what they already suspected.

I seem to frequently have issues with common social conventions.

For example...

You know how hotels fold the first piece of toilet paper in your bathroom into a point? Yeah, I can't use that piece because I know someone else touched it.

I almost always go the wrong way for a hug and end up cracking heads with the person. I'm definitely awkward when it comes to hugs. Recently at a wedding, someone I didn't know came in for a hug. Hugging strangers is awkward enough for me, but she was wearing one of those dresses where her shoulders and back were completely bare. Um, where are you supposed to put your hands when hugging someone who has no clothing on their back? I do not know the rules for this, so I just left my hands where they were, in my pockets, and let her hug me. It probably seemed rude, but I couldn't figure out what else to do in time. I'm so thankful I don't live in Italy, because I can't even imagine all the problems I'd have with the whole cheek-kissing thing.

I can't get myself to use LOL in a text message (unless I'm being sarcastic). It seems like that one should be reserved exclusively for middle school girls, right? I'm going to stick with "Ha!" which has exactly the same number of characters and doesn't look like my daughter is texting from my phone.

I get all skeptical when someone says, "You're in our thoughts and prayers." What does that even mean? Probably something like, "I see you right now, so I'm going to say something nice to you. Later when I don't see you, I won't be thinking about you or praying for you—you poor little fella."

I take the "most awkward person in the room award" when someone leads us in a moment of silence. I "so" don't know what to do. Usually, I start by wondering about how long this moment will last. Then I move on to thinking about what everyone else might be thinking or doing during the moment of silence. Finally, I run out of thoughts and get impatient. Sometimes I even start wishing someone will mess it up with accidental sounds. Terrible, I know.

And then there's the expression "rest in peace." I've always had issues with this one. At first, I just felt uncomfortable with it and didn't quite know the rules that govern how the saying should be used. I figured it was mostly acceptable on tombstones and memorial tattoos, but other than that, I had no idea.

Even though I can see it is common on tombstones and tattoos, I still have lots of questions...

Does saying it (rest in peace) do anything?

Isn't it too late to wish for a better or more pleasant outcome for the individual now?

Does R.I.P. even jibe with the Christian faith?

Aren't we doing stuff in Heaven—like more than just resting and having peace?

And if the person isn't in Heaven, is there really any hope for peace or rest?

Is rest and peace something only available for the afterlife—like we all have to wait until we die to get some?

If rest and peace is only for the afterlife, what does that say about now? "You're alive, so no peace and no rest. It's just not allowed." Really?

SHOUT-OUTS

I've had this uncomfortable feeling about "rest in peace" for a while.

Then, one day while working with Yogi Bear Sunday School in Brooklyn, I really got slapped in the face with R.I.P.

We had spent the morning on bus routes, picking up thousands of adorable elementary-aged kids from the surrounding neighborhoods. These kids were beautiful and street-smart. They were precious and tough. They could sing like angels, and they knew all the lyrics to 50 Cent's "In Da Club" (not the edited radio version either).

Yogi Bear Sunday School was about to begin. We packed into the bleachers with the kids. Music was blaring and the lights were on. What looked like hundreds of prizes straight out of Toys-R-Us lined the stage. The eyes of the kids were wide with excitement and the room was buzzing.

Two staff members were roaming around with microphones, asking, "Who wants to give a shout-out?" Hands waved everywhere, and a few lucky kids got their moment in the spotlight.

Shout-outs were given to moms and older brothers and sisters. I think there were even a few shout-outs for candy and Coca-Cola.

A seven year-old boy on the bleachers a few rows behind me was selected. His name was Anjawon and he now had the mic. "I wanna give a shout out to my cousin Demondre, may he rest in peace." Then he did that gesture where he touched his lips, his heart, and finished by pointing to the sky while looking up.

I was in shock. We went from kid shout-outs about candy and moms to a R.I.P. moment for a cousin who died before his time. Maybe what threw me the most was how confidently Anjawon used the "rest in peace" expression. This seven year-old said it with the accompanying hand motions in a way that I never could.

For the rest of that day, I couldn't stop thinking about Anjawon's R.I.P. shout-out for his cousin Demondre. Was Demondre's life so difficult and stressful that death is now a blessing—a reward of peace and rest for all the hardships he'd been through?

Do I just have a bad attitude about R.I.P.?

Maybe I should see what the Bible has to say about it.

It's pretty embarrassing to admit that I was 30-something before I even knew that the R.I.P. expression actually comes from the Bible. Whoops! Somehow I missed that one in Bible college.

Here's the verse where R.I.P. comes from:

"For those who follow godly paths will rest in peace when they die." (Isaiah 57.2 NLT)

OK, so it's biblical—I can certainly appreciate that. Looks like I will have to back down. I'm not going to look critically at tombstones or memorial tattoos anymore.

Of course, there is a specific context in which the Isaiah 57 passage was written. Good people were dying before their time because of violence and injustice, and evil leaders were doing nothing about it.

But there's something here that we need to understand: something big, something subversive and quite strange compared to how things work in our world...

God wants us to have peace and rest long before we "rest in peace."

That's what this book is all about: saying "no thank you" to the world's way of strain and stress while embracing God's gift of peace and rest; not waiting for peace and rest until we R.I.P.

"My people will live in peaceful places and in safe homes and in calm places of rest." (Isaiah 32.18 NCV)

God's plan is for us to LIVE in peaceful places, in calm places of rest.

He has a life of peace and rest for us before we R.I.P.

CHAPTER 4 BIG IDEAS

There's something here that we need to understand: something big, something subversive and quite strange compared to how things work in our world...

God wants us to have peace and rest long before we "rest in peace."

That's what this book is all about: saying "no thank you" to the world's way of strain and stress while embracing God's gift of peace and rest; not waiting for peace and rest until we R.I.P.

"My people will live in peaceful places and in safe homes and in calm places of rest." (Isaiah 32.18 NCV)

God's plan is for us to LIVE in peaceful places, in calm places of rest.

QUESTIONS
FOR INDIVIDUAL &/OR GROUP STUDY

1. What normal social conventions do you struggle with and cause you to be all awkward?

2. What have you thought about the meaning of R.I.P.?

3. What does saying "no thank you" to the world's way of strain and stress look like, practically speaking?

4. What are some ways we can embrace God's gift of peace and rest now?

5. Does living in "peaceful places and in safe homes" mean that all God's people should live in gated communities with security and alarms? What do you think it means?

6. Describe what "calm places of rest" look like in your life. Are you getting enough?

R.I.P.

Come to me. I'll take care of you, protect you.
Calm, calm down. You're exhausted, come lie down.
You don't have to explain, I understand.
—Björk (Come to Me)

Come to me, all of you who are weary and carry heavy burdens, and I will give you rest.
—Jesus (Matthew 11.28 NLT)

5. RECIPIENTS

I look just like my dad (well, actually I'm a slightly younger and tiny bit more handsome version of him). I have the same male pattern baldness, skinny legs, chubby belly, blue eyes...

And this is not my doing, except for maybe the chubby belly part.

I received these genes.

Actually, there's a lot I've received from my dad—more than just DNA...

His love of ice cream and his popcorn making skills.

His habit of yelling at the TV while watching football.

His eagerness to take long road trips and be the only driver.

His steady, hard-working, faithful disposition.

My wife even says I have his walk, whatever that means.

One of the most distinguishing marks of the Christian faith is that it is something received, not achieved, earned, accomplished, or attained. This makes Jesus the Hero of the story, and not us.

The common thread of religion is the message: "Work harder, do better, try some more, improve yourself, climb the ladder, with all this effort you're really going somewhere now."

Religion is stressful. Think about it...

Religion always has another 3 points to become something-or-other. It prods and pushes. Instead of lightening the load, it heaps on another serving of religious duty, and the weight becomes unbearable.

The message of Jesus goes against the grain of typical religion. Instead of "do more and try harder" Jesus simply said, "Come to me, and I will give you rest." Religion tends to be about achieving while the Kingdom of God is about receiving. In the Christian faith, God does all the heavy lifting. Our job is to trust and receive.

We are recipients.

PEACE AND REST GIVEN NOW

The Message Bible shows the clear contrast between Kingdom of God ways and typical religion...

"Are you tired? Worn out? Burned out on religion? Come to me. Get away with me and you'll recover your life. I'll show you how to take a real rest. Walk with me and work with me—watch how I do it. Learn the unforced rhythms of grace. I won't lay anything heavy or ill-fitting on you. Keep company with me and you'll learn to live freely and lightly." (Matthew 11.28-30 MSG)

Taking it even further, Jesus exposed those who were behind religion's message of "Do more and try harder" when He said, "You're hopeless, you religion scholars! You load people down with rules and regulations, nearly breaking their backs, but never lift even a finger to help." (Luke 11.46 MSG)

Jesus didn't come to load people down with more weight, but to lift burdens and give rest. He came to serve and to give. "I came not to be served but to serve and to give my life for you." (Matthew 20.28 paraphrased)

Our job is to trust Him and receive.

I must say, I'm no expert or guru about anything really. I haven't reached some Zen-like status of peace and rest. Rather, I'm a recipient. And that's what I want to share with you...

The Good News about what God has done for us and has given to us.

So this book isn't about self-help tips. Instead, it's a reminder or announcement of what God has available for us NOW—before we're buried.

Yes, actually right now, God has peace and rest for us.

That's what I'm announcing. Or maybe I'm reminding you of something you already know. Either way, I'm going to say it again and hopefully inspire you to actually believe it. God wants us to have peace and rest now, in this life.

It's not about a quest for peace and rest. We're not seeking or pursuing it; we are simply receiving. We are recipients of the Kingdom life and Kingdom ways. We accept His counter-cultural, subversive way of living with all its Kingdom benefits. This makes us a little bit strange and easy to identify—like foreigners living in another country.

IDENTIFIABLY STRANGE

Recently, while spending a month living in the Italian countryside, I was constantly aware of how much we stood out. Our strangeness was completely obvious to the locals...

All three of us have blue eyes and pale skin.

We talk like cowboys. I never thought I sounded like a cowboy before, but after hearing an Italian say "ristorante" I was struck with how beautiful, romantic, and poetic the word sounded. Then I said "restaurant" and realized that I could have spit a big wad of tobacco out of my mouth and it would've fit perfectly.

We buy ten times the amount of groceries. One day, we went to the same store three times. All their products are packaged in cute little containers (which I think is why Italians are cute and little too). Yeah, people stared at us in the market, and I think I detected smirks on their faces.

When you pay for something in Italy and the cashier has change to give you, they place it in a little change tray on the counter. We are not used to that at all. Every time we expected change, we would stick a hand out waiting for them to put some change in it, and every time, the cashier would bypass the hand and place the change in the tray. It's rather embarrassing, like a missed high-five or an unwanted kiss.

At one point, I noticed all three of us had our iPhones out. We were together physically, but totally engrossed in our electronic devices. Distinctly American.

Our clothing and shoes revealed who we were. The touristy maps sold us out. Our strangeness was conspicuous in Italy.

Kingdom of God people are strange too, at least in the eyes of the world. There are dead giveaways—not because of accents or fashion or diet, but because of something more internal.

We run on a different set of core beliefs, priorities, and values...

Our attitude is strange (in a wonderful way).

We are Good News people in a bad news world.

We are full of joy even when life is hard.

We are unshakable.

No matter how dark it gets, we're always the people of hope.

We aren't pushing our way to the top, but instead, we're happy to serve and put ourselves out for others.

We aren't wasting time living angry. God has been too good to us for that.

We love people, all people. No strings attached. We love because He loved us first.

We don't obsess over politics because we serve The King and we're part of His Kingdom.

What we have received from God is so incredibly amazing, we just can't keep it to ourselves. We've got to share it!

Religious people tend to make things strange externally, through special clothing and vocabulary, and hairstyles... outward things.

Jesus didn't do that. He looked like everyone else. He spent time hanging out with regular people. He spoke in the common, everyday language. He didn't stand out because of his appearance or circle of friends or special vocabulary.

In fact, when Judas sold Jesus out, he had to indicate to the soldiers which person Jesus was in the crowd. Judas kissed Jesus on the cheek, identifying Him as the one to arrest. Jesus didn't look different from everyone else; He didn't have a messiah hair cut or special clothing. He was certainly strange, but not because of external things.

Yes, Kingdom of God people are easily identifiable. We stand out. Even though we shop at the same stores, wear the same clothes, and listen to the same music, something is different about us and people notice. Our strangeness is obvious. In fact, I'm pretty sure some of them are smirking at us right now.

CHAPTER 5 BIG IDEAS

"Come to me, all of you who are weary and carry heavy burdens, and I will give you rest." (Matthew 11.28 NLT)

One of the most distinguishing marks of the Christian faith is that it is something received, not achieved, earned, accomplished, or attained. This makes Jesus the Hero of the story, and not us.

We are recipients. Our job is to trust Him and receive.

God wants us to have peace and rest now, in this life.

It's not about a quest for peace and rest. We're not seeking or pursuing it; we are simply receiving. We are recipients of the Kingdom life and Kingdom ways. We accept His counter-cultural, subversive way of living with all its Kingdom benefits.

Kingdom of God people are strange, at least in the eyes of the world. There are dead giveaways—not because of accents or fashion or diet, but because of something more internal.

QUESTIONS
FOR INDIVIDUAL &/OR GROUP STUDY

1. What are some things you've "received" from your family?

2. What happens to Christianity when the emphasis moves away from us being recipients to us working our way towards something?

3. In what ways have you experienced the heavy weight of religion?

4. In what ways have you experienced the liberating load-lifting of coming to Jesus?

5. What are some ways religion becomes strange externally?

6. What are some ways Kingdom of God people are strange internally?

I only miss you when I'm breathing.
I only need you when my heart is beating.
You are the color that I'm bleeding. I only miss you when I'm breathing.
—Jason DeRulo (Breathing)

True to Your word, You let me catch my breath and send me in the right direction.
—David (Psalm 23.3 MSG)

6. PERCENTAGE

I once took a "stress test" that asked whether certain major stressful events happened in the past year of my life. To my surprise, I had to answer "yes" to 90% of the questions. Some of the major stressful events included:

Relocating
Death of a family member
Selling and/or purchasing a home
Change of career
Getting married

There were only a few items on the list that didn't apply to me (like divorce, death of a spouse, and bankruptcy). At the time, I felt like I had a lot going on. I don't think I would have described myself as stressed out, but my pace of life was definitely taxing.

Some things in life can only be sustained for so long. Sure, in college we study and work and play and function on three or four hours of sleep a night, but we know we can't continue at that pace forever. Functioning on too little peace and rest will eventually hurt us.

You're probably somewhat familiar with the story of Job, right? You know, the dude who had it all and then lost it all in a terrible turn of events. He suffered for a season, and eventually rebounded higher than he ever was before.

During his suffering season, Job was absolutely miserable. It wasn't that he had his luxury car repossessed and his home taken over by the bank so he had to lower his standard of living drastically...

No, Job lost all of his children in a tragic accident and his own health declined to the point where he wished he could die.

While deep in his suffering season, Job said, "I have no peace, no rest, and my troubles never end." (Job 3.26 GNT)

What an awful place to be—where there is no peace and no rest.

We're talking about the complete absence of peace and rest. There's another way of describing this: it's called hell.

"And the smoke of their torment ascends forever and ever; and they have no respite (no pause, no intermission, no rest, no peace) day or night." (Revelation 14.11 AMP)

No peace, no break, no rest. Welcome to hell.

I've often wondered - how long was Job's season of suffering?

The Bible doesn't tell us specifically. Job did say, "Month after month I have nothing to live for; night after night brings me grief." (Job 7.3 GNT). So we presume his suffering lasted some months. Jewish tradition says Job suffered for twelve months.

BREAKDOWN

Perhaps a more important question to consider is - how long can we go without peace or rest? It seems obvious that we need some. But how much do we need? How often?

I remember learning in school about the industrial revolution. Machines and factories increased productivity to new and previously unimagined levels. Work was able to happen around the clock, seven days a week.

But something else began to happen: breakdown. That pace wasn't sustainable—not for humans or machines. We just can't function forever without rest.

God established the pattern for us: for six days He created, and on the seventh day He rested. Interesting, isn't it? I don't believe God needed the rest. He wasn't exhausted, out-of-breath, depleted, or worn-out. He was showing us the way.

God actually commanded the Israelites to refrain from working on the Sabbath—the seventh day. It was to be a legislated "day of rest." One out of seven. That's like 14%.

And think about a 24 hour period. There's about eight hours of darkness. That's 33%. Even for people who only sleep six hours a night, that's still 25% of the whole day. Apparently God thinks we need rest on such a regular basis that He built "lights out" into the system.

There are some things we just cannot function without—like water and oxygen. The air we breathe is about 21% oxygen. At high altitudes, that percentage decreases. At about 5% oxygen, the body's vital organs begin to shut down. We weren't designed to function on that low of a percentage of oxygen.

Similarly, we need peace and rest. We weren't created to sustain an existence with too low of a percentage of peace and rest in our lives.

We need peace and rest like we need oxygen and water. When we don't have enough of them, we function poorly, and without them, we won't last long. The complete absence of peace and rest in our lives? That's hell.

A few years ago, my wife and I hiked the Grand Canyon (it was her idea). I was pretty nervous about the whole thing. Shari read up on the hike and made sure we had everything we needed.

Of all the things emphasized by the Park Rangers to keep you safe while hiking the canyon, can you guess what was at the top of their list?

I thought it should be something like, "Don't fall off the cliff!" Or maybe, "Come back when you're in better shape." But it wasn't. It wasn't even "Watch out for rattlesnakes!" The number one thing all the signs and literature said was, "Bring lots of water—even more than you think you need."

Apparently they have more people who end up needing to be rescued because of dehydration than because of falling off the cliffs or fainting from exhaustion or being bit by poisonous snakes.

BIG PLAYS

By the way, have you ever noticed what football players do on the sidelines after making huge plays? Yeah, I know, they high-five, chest bump, and get their rears patted...

But eventually, they sit down on the bench and put on an oxygen mask.

Why?

Because, after big plays, they need some recovery time.

Oxygen and water.

Peace and rest.

Nobody can keep going without them. We all need a healthy percentage in our lives.

I'll go out on a limb and suggest most of us have been functioning with not enough peace and rest in our lives. We need more.

It's a good thing God is our never-ending source for all that we need.

CHAPTER 6 BIG IDEAS

"True to Your word, You let me catch my breath and send me in the right direction." (Psalm 23.3 MSG)

Some things in life can only be sustained for so long. Functioning on too little peace and rest will eventually hurt us.

Apparently God thinks we need rest on such a regular basis that He built "lights out" into the system.

We need peace and rest like we need oxygen and water. When we don't have enough of them, we function poorly, and without them, we won't last long. The complete absence of peace and rest in our lives? That's hell.

Most of us have been functioning with not enough peace and rest in our lives. We need more.

It's a good thing God is our never-ending source for all that we need.

QUESTIONS
FOR INDIVIDUAL &/OR GROUP STUDY

1. How do you think you would do on a stress test right now? What are some of the "taxing" things going on in your life?

2. Perhaps not to the scale of Job's, but have you gone through a "suffering season" before? Did you feel a complete absence of peace and rest? How long did it last?

3. How has functioning on too little peace and rest hurt you?

4. Think about some "big plays" you had that were great, but also demanded extra peace and rest afterwards.

5. What does extra peace and rest look like for you?

6. How does God being our source encourage you when you are running on empty?

And my head keeps spinning.
Can't stop having these visions, I gotta get with it.
 —Kanye West (Welcome to Heartbreak)

We hoped for peace, but no peace came.
—Jeremiah (Jeremiah 8.15 NLT)

7. PEACELESS

My daughter regularly asks, "Daddy, will you tell me a story about when you were little?" I have my favorites and go-to's when she asks. I like to tell her stories that are interesting and funny. The easiest ones come from my 9 years of working at the veterinary hospital in South Seattle (I have visual aids, scars to go along with the stories).

She also asks my mom to tell her stories about when I was younger. I'm not sure if she's looking for inconsistencies between the stories to catch me revising history and exaggerating, or if she's hoping to hear something she's never heard before. Actually, I'm pretty sure there's a little bit of both going on.

Frequently, my daughter will come home from a visit with my parents and say, "You know what Grammy told me?!!?!!"

Great. I know what this means—another story from my childhood that I'd rather not have my daughter knowing or talking about.

My mom loves to tell the story of when I was in kindergarten...

On this particular day, my mom thought she might be home five minutes later than when I would be arriving home from school, so she sent me with a key and instructions to let myself in if she wasn't there yet.

I'll admit it: I'm a mama's boy. I was terrified. The idea that I would have to spend five minutes alone at home without my mom had me worried.

I worried the whole time I was at school that my mom wouldn't be home and I would be all alone. After school, I arrived at our house and knocked on the door like I usually did—hoping my mom would be there to open it. But there was nothing. My worst fears were realized.

It didn't take long for me to start crying. OK, I was probably crying even before I knocked, worried that I would be all alone.

What I didn't know, is that my mom WAS HOME. She was in a back bedroom and didn't hear my first knock. But by the time she made it to the front door, I was in full force, wailing...

"Oh, no! Where's my Mommy? What am I going to do?"

She stood at the door listening, completely entertained (I still think this is evil).

According to the story my mother tells my daughter, the wailing at the front door went on for a few minutes. "Where's my Mommy? What am I going to do? Oh, no!"

Now, I don't remember all this. I do remember being scared and feeling abandoned, but I don't recall the loud wailing part. Maybe I blocked that out of my memory banks. Or maybe my mom exaggerates. Probably.

Eventually, my mom realized her entertainment was at my expense (and was evil), so she opened the door to welcome me home. All was right in the world. My tears stopped flowing and I wailed no more.

ALL GROWN UP NOW

I'm sure this is my mom's all-time favorite story from my growing-up years.

And I can see why. It's funny.

I got caught saying out loud what I was thinking and feeling on the inside, which is pretty cute coming from a child...

But imagine how embarrassing that would be now as an adult!

The thing is, my fears and worries really aren't much different today. Sure, I'm more sophisticated now. I'm not going to let the neighbors catch me wailing.

The truth is, deep down, I'm still that little boy who fears abandonment. When I'm insecure and unsure about life, I still want to know, "Where's my Mommy?" And life's circumstances often cause me to cry out (on the inside), "Oh, no! What am I going to do?"

Functioning with no peace creates big problems in our lives.

It causes decline...

Our relationships suffer. It's practically impossible to bring something positive and healthy to a relationship when there's an absence of peace in your heart.

We struggle with ourselves. When we don't have peace, we're not happy with anything or anyone—including ourselves. We become our own worst enemies: insecure, self-loathing, and constantly dissatisfied.

We project onto God. Our own fears, worries, and insecurities turn God into more of a monster than a loving Father. How we see God says a lot about what's going on in our hearts. Have you ever considered what's really going on in the hearts of the Westboro Baptist gang of angry protestors?

Eventually, we turn into dog-eat-dog, vengeful, paranoid, delusional, angry, stressed-out, super negative people.

Doesn't sound like something anybody wants for themselves.

The absence of peace makes our heads spin. We become drunk on our own "what if" visions and can't see straight anymore.

It's funny how we can lose peace over the unknown.

In my kindergarten doorstep story, the whole time I was at school, I worried about my mom being gone. Then, when I arrived home, I was convinced that my worst fears had been realized. Except that I was wrong.

I spent half my day experiencing no peace over something that wasn't even true.

This isn't just a childhood thing. I still find myself doing this.

THE LORD OF PEACE

When I think about my first few years of leading our church, well, let's just say I did some wailing on the inside. It was a time of transition and change. I was adapting to the new role. The church was doing its best to adapt to me.

There was a lot of movement. People were coming and people were going.

And when long-time, leadership-type, "big-giving" members of the church left because of me, I felt like my kindergarten self all over again. I was losing sleep. My stomach hurt from worrying. I was crying on the inside, "Oh, no! What am I going to do? Where's my Mommy?"

I wasn't saying it out loud on the doorstep, but I felt it out loud in my heart. I spent significant amounts of time experiencing no peace over "what if" scenarios that proved to not even be true.

Now, looking back, it's easy to think, "What a waste of time and energy. Why were you so worried about that? It all turned out for the best, you silly kid!"

But in those moments, when you're standing on the doorstep knocking and your mommy doesn't answer right away, what do you do?

Is it possible to have peace even when life is uncertain and it seems like there's more to worry about than there is to be confident about?

Paul thought so. He said, "May the Lord of peace Himself give you His peace at all times and in every situation." (2 Thessalonians 3.16 NLT).

I love that.

May the Lord of peace Himself give you His peace at all times and in every situation.

The Lord of peace.

Giving us His peace.

At all times and in every situation.

CHAPTER 7 BIG IDEAS

"We hoped for peace, but no peace came." (Jeremiah 8.15 NLT)

My fears and worries really aren't much different today. The truth is, deep down, I'm still that little boy who fears abandonment. When I'm insecure and unsure about life, I still want to know, "Where's my Mommy?" And life's circumstances often cause me to cry out (on the inside), "Oh, no! What am I going to do?"

The absence of peace makes our heads spin. We become drunk on our own "what if" visions and can't see straight anymore.

Functioning with no peace creates big problems in our lives.

It's funny how we can lose peace over the unknown.

Is it possible to have peace even when life is uncertain and it seems like there's more to worry about than there is to be confident about? Paul thought so. He said, "May the Lord of peace Himself give you His peace at all times and in every situation." (2 Thessalonians 3.16 NLT).

QUESTIONS
FOR INDIVIDUAL &/OR GROUP STUDY

1. What is your favorite story of when you were younger?

2. How have your greatest fears changed from when you were 5 years old compared to now?

3. How many of your greatest fears have been realized?

4. Have you had some "what if" visions that caused you to not be able to see straight?

5. When have you lost peace over the unknown?

6. When have you experienced God's "peace at all times and in every situation?"

You know what the Midwest is? Young and restless.
—Kanye West (Jesus Walks)

There's no rest in the west.
—Bob Marley (The Oppressed Song)

Too much activity gives you restless dreams.
—Solomon (Ecclesiastes 5.3 NLT)

8. RESTLESS

Several years ago, my wife and I went on a vacation with some family members in La Paz, Mexico. I was looking forward to resting and soaking up some sunshine.

La Paz seemed less touristy than other places we had been in Mexico before and I liked that. The hotel was nice and the pool was absolutely perfect.

At dinner we did our best to interpret the menus written in Spanish.

Pizza seemed like a safe option, and I'm always up for some pizza, so my wife ordered her favorite – "Hawaiian." When the pizza came out, we had a real mystery before us. What exactly was on this pizza? It had some strange, unidentifiable toppings. A few bites in, we discovered the distinct flavors of BANANA and MARASCHINO CHERRIES along with the pineapple and ham. That was the first and last time we've had that variation of the Hawaiian pizza.

The family wanted to go on an excursion, so we booked a private beach and snorkeling boat trip. It sounded wonderfully refreshing to me—like what vacations are supposed to provide: a healthy dose of peace and rest.

When it was time for us to board the boat, I sensed something was wrong. It looked like we had purchased tickets for a small fishing boat. Everyone else was smiling and getting on board, but I kept thinking this had to be the wrong boat. I scanned the beach for a more appropriate looking vessel but there was none.

We stepped on to what was basically a metal rowboat with an outboard motor attached to the back. It soon became evident that our "captain" didn't speak a word of English. As we motored away from shore, I had a growing sense of unrest.

SAFETY VIOLATIONS

I looked around...

No life vests. No radio. No cell phones. No life ring. No safety kit. No flare gun. No oars. No spare gas can. No GPS. No ability to communicate with the captain. My family members all seemed oblivious to the expansive list of blatant safety violations on this boating trip.

Although the scenery around us was beautiful, I didn't even notice. I was focused on being concerned for our lives.

Our captain took us 30 minutes away from shore. I knew this was much farther than I could swim. My life was in the hands of the captain (who, by the way, wasn't wearing a uniform or badge and none of us knew his name).

We approached a tiny little island—which I think might have been the same uninhabited island that Tom Hanks was stranded on in the movie "Cast Away."

This is where we were stopping for the day??!!!?! As we got off the boat, I looked around. There wasn't even a volleyball here. Wow. Tom Hanks had it better than us.

I wondered if we would be stranded here forever. I kept a close watch on the captain because I was concerned he might take off without us.

My vigilant watch continued through the day while my family members swam and played on the beach. Much to my relief, as the sun began to set, it was finally time for us to take off. I hoped we had enough fuel to get us back to shore.

Just as I was feeling a little bit better, the motor cut out. Was this it? Were we going to die at sea in a metal rowboat?

The captain had turned off the motor because this was a good place to snorkel (I knew this because the captain pretended to put a mask on, smiled, pointed to us and the water, then made some swimming gestures). My naïve family members all started jumping into the water with their snorkel gear on.

SWIMMING WITH SEA COWS

They began pressuring me to join them. Swirling in my mind was a bunch of important questions...

Was this rented snorkel gear sanitized?

Are we certain there aren't sharks out here?

Will the captain leave us once we all jump in?

Against my better judgment, I caved in to their pressure and jumped in.

Within two minutes of being in the water, I noticed that we were surrounded by a herd of manatees. These things are huge (they weigh about 1,000 pounds and they're sometimes called sea cows). This particular herd seemed to have some kind of skin disease going on.

They were very interested in us and instead of swimming away, they came in for a closer look...

So close, in fact, that they started brushing up against us. One touched me and that was it. I'd had enough. This was my breaking point. Three minutes in the water was all I could handle with these mangy sea cows touching me.

I got back in the boat and sat silently with the captain for 45 minutes while my family finished up their afternoon of swimming with the cows.

NEED A VACATION

When we finally arrived back to the shore, I was the first one to jump out of the boat. It was such a relief to have our little boating excursion behind us.

What a stressful day! This vacation was exhausting. I felt like I needed a vacation from this vacation.

Somehow I had twisted what should have been restful and relaxing into something stressful and exhausting. I was unable to rest, relax, recharge, or enjoy the day because I couldn't (or wouldn't) turn my brain off.

Restlessness, or the absence of rest, causes problems in our lives.

Without rest, we become drained and weary. We lose our sense of drive and ambition. Our vision becomes blurry. We get clumsy and have more frequent failures. Lack of rest typically leads to bad decision-making.

When we are deprived of rest, we get sick: physically, emotionally, and spiritually.

And when that happens, we are sometimes forced to rest.

I like the imagery of the 23rd Psalm. In talking about God as our shepherd, it says, "He MAKES ME lie down in green pastures."

God wants us to have rest. He gives us rest.

He even built eight hours of "lights out" into the system so we would rest.

Occasionally, He might even have to make us rest.

CHAPTER 8 BIG IDEAS

"Too much activity gives you restless dreams." (Ecclesiastes 5.3 NLT)

Restlessness, or the absence of rest, causes problems in our lives.

Without rest, we become drained and weary. We lose our sense of drive and ambition. Our vision becomes blurry. We get clumsy and have more frequent failures. Lack of rest typically leads to bad decision-making.

When we are deprived of rest, we get sick: physically, emotionally, and spiritually.

And when that happens, we are sometimes forced to rest.

God wants us to have rest. He gives us rest.

QUESTIONS
FOR INDIVIDUAL &/OR GROUP STUDY

1. Have you ever had a bad vacation experience? Or bad pizza?

2. What is a restful activity or experience for you that may not be restful for others?

3. What problems has the absence of rest caused in your life?

4. Have you experienced getting sick (physically, emotionally, or spiritually) from lack of rest? How did you recover?

5. Has there been a time when you experienced "forced" rest? What was that like?

6. How does God give you rest?

Tryina keep it clean like church clothes.
—Lupe Fiasco (I Don't Wanna Care Right Now)

Do you want to stand out? Then step down. Be a servant. If you're content to simply be yourself, your life will count for plenty.
—Jesus (Matthew 23.11-12 MSG)

9. CHURCHIFIED

From day one, I've been in the church. Even when I was taking drugs and being an angst-filled, little punk rock skateboarder kid, I still went to church (because my parents made me). I never really had a choice. It wasn't just my parents who had a plan for me to be in church; I think God had something to do with it too.

During my rebellious years, I went on a bit of a reign of terror in the church. It became my playground for practical jokes. Some of my greatest hits were...

Sliding parked cars around in the gravel parking lot so that they were too close to each other and impossible to open any of their doors (not by myself—I'm not strong enough, but with 3 other guys, we could easily move smaller cars wherever we wanted them).

Breaking into the youth pastor's office, and pushing all of his furniture against the inside of his door, then sneaking out the window.

Emptying a whole box of Goldfish crackers found in the nursery into the baptismal tank before the Sunday evening baptism service.

Yes, I know I was terrible. Truth is, I still am.

And despite all my mischief and mayhem, I love the church—and I'm convinced the church loves me back.

THE CHURCH'S G.P.A.

I've never not been involved in church. It's all I've ever known. Sure, it has some strange, weird, and embarrassing features, but so do I and so does my family. Don't we all?

There's not much I haven't seen when it comes to church and church life. If you think you have a shocking or beyond-belief story about church, I'm 99% sure it won't surprise me at all.

In fact, I've probably been there, done that—and bought the T-shirt, or sweatshirt. In the '80's, I proudly wore my youth group's sweatshirt with our name painted across the front in neon pink.

What was the youth group's name?

R.A.D.D.

Yeah, that's right. We were the Renton Assembly Devil Defeaters.

See what I mean? Been there, done that—bought the sweatshirt too.

I've experienced more church potlucks, Christian skate nights, sweaty summer Bible camps, revival meetings, testimony nights, missionary presentations, guest speakers, offertories (this is a very "special" song during the offering usually sung karaoke-style), church business meetings, Easter plays, work parties, prayer meetings, small groups, singing Christmas trees, retreats, and Sunday nights after church at Shakey's Pizza than I can count.

Some of these experiences I am profoundly grateful for because they were key in the shaping of who I am today. Others, well... let's just say I survived them. And there are a few experiences I'm still trying to scrub from my memory bank.

Even with all her imperfections, I'm absolutely in love with the church. I've never been more excited about the future. God is using us, His church, to announce Good News everywhere and love people the way He does. We are bright lights shining in the darkness.

Here's what I mean by bright lights shining:

We are subversive in ways that bless, encourage, strengthen, and communicate love through action.

We are leaving people surprised by grace and baffled by the blessing, causing them to wonder, "Who does stuff like this?"

Just recently, someone was asking me about our 5pm service where we throw a party, provide dinner for everyone, and give away free bags of groceries. The guy looked at me, totally surprised, and said, "Wait, you mean you do this EVERY week?"

He couldn't believe what I was telling him. It just seemed too good to be true. He was surprised by grace, baffled by the blessing, and wondered, "Who does stuff like this?"

Not too long ago, we had some thieves show up at our church on a Sunday morning. They sat in the service, looking for opportunities to be successful in their line of work. And they were successful. They stole some purses and a car.

Here's where it gets interesting...

They got caught later in the week by the police. A few people in our church had attended school with the thieves and knew them - so they reached out to them. They offered the thieves forgiveness, help, gave them rides, and invited them back to church.

The lady who had her purse and car stolen by the thieves went up to them in church, smiled, and gave them big hugs. The thieves were sobbing - ashamed and embarrassed. But the church lady said, "Oh, you don't need to cry! You're forgiven. I'm just happy to see you today."

Now that's unusual.

Darkness is usual: fear, anger, blame, accusation, pointing the finger, giving the finger, and having an "us -vs- them" attitude.

Light shines out in the darkness, declaring: "You are loved, wanted, accepted, and welcomed home as family."

It is generous beyond what is reasonable.

A couple of years ago at our Great Big Backpack Give, we ran out of backpacks and school supplies in about 30 minutes, so we started turning people away. A volunteer at the event saw what was happening, went to those families who didn't get backpacks or school supplies - and she promised to buy them everything personally. Those families met her on Sunday at church and she gave them all they needed.

Serious, who does stuff like this?

Kingdom of God people do. We announce Good News everywhere and love people the way He does. We are bright lights shining in the darkness.

THE KINGDOM MESSAGE

It's true that church has never been perfect.

There has not been a time in church history when we got a 4.0 grade point average and I don't expect it to happen anytime soon. We are stained and full of flaws, yet God continues to use us (which reminds us once again that He is the Hero of the story, not us).

The church gets a lot right. We also have a lot of things backwards.

Jesus said, "Come to me, all of you who are weary and carry heavy burdens, and I will give you rest," but I think the church's message often sounds the opposite—something like this, "Come to us on Sunday morning and we will give you stress."

If we're giving people guilt-trips, impossible religious standards that even the pastors and leaders aren't keeping up with, and a long list of tips on how to do more and be better, we have it backwards.

The Kingdom Message is one of peace and rest...

It announces that although we were once enemies with God because of our sin, He chooses to reconcile us to Himself. We are no longer enemies; instead we are friends. We have peace with God—not because of anything we've done, but because of what He has done for us.

It declares, "It is finished." God has done all the heavy lifting for us. We can rest in Him, knowing that He loves us perfectly and nothing will ever change that. God is good with us, and we can be too. Finally all the straining and stressing to gain His approval can be put to rest.

On both points, God is the Hero. He does the reconciling. He paid our debt in full. We have nothing to prove, earn, pay, or show. Our job is to trust Him and receive.

When we aren't the hero of the story, we get no credit and we don't take the blame. This is incredibly freeing...

And yet, the whole "no credit" thing goes totally against our nature. Sure, we don't want the blame, but credit is something we all want.

The thing is, if we take the credit, we're writing ourselves in as the hero of the story again, which also means we're signing up to take the blame. We can't have it both ways. We have to decide: who is the hero of our story?

How our churches act and sound reveals our choice on the matter. When we...

Get all churchified
Keep up a frantic pace
Are addicted to the "lights, camera, action" show

Build on the cult of personality, creating Christian celebrities
Struggle to get excited over the simple and little things
Get starry-eyed over experts and gurus
Take ourselves seriously
Strain and strive

The hero has been chosen. It's not Him, the hero is us.

GIMMICKS, TRICKS, AND STRATEGIES

This is when things get really funky in the church. It kind of reminds me of the story of the prophets of Baal in a showdown with Elijah. They wanted their god to respond to their prayers, so they prayed and prayed for hours. They increased their volume and intensity. They danced and sweat and even bled a little. These guys were having some serious "church."

But with all their intensity and spiritual fervor what actually happened? Not a thing.

"They used every religious trick and strategy they knew to make something happen on the altar, but nothing happened—not so much as a whisper, not a flicker of response." (I Kings 18.29 MSG)

I wonder how often this describes our attempts to make things happen? Every religious trick and strategy, every gimmick and marketing method invented...

Sadly, I think it happens a lot.

Elijah, on the other hand, was peaceful, quiet, and at rest. His prayer was simple, not flashy. His first request? "Let it be known today that You are God." (1 Kings 18.36 NIV).

Elijah was basically saying, "God, you're the Hero of the story. Do what you do, I'm your servant."

Often, our churchified selves depend more on upping the ante, increasing the intensity, straining and stressing to do more in order to make something happen...

Do more. Work harder. Try again. Climb the ladder.

We shout and we dance and we sweat and we even bleed a little. But nothing's happening. Why? Because fruit is never the result of gimmicks, tricks, and strategies.

THANKFUL & EMBARRASSED

The real fruit and the best results always come from that quiet place of confidence in the Hero, where we have true peace and rest.

In fact, I believe fruitfulness follows peace and rest. Selah (pause and think about that for a moment).

Having been in the ministry for over 20 years now, when I reflect back on what I've said and done, I am equally thankful and embarrassed...

I'm thankful for the relationships built and the opportunity to invest in the lives of others. I'm thankful that, despite all my quirks and weaknesses, God still chose me to be a leader in His church. I'm thankful for all the leaders who have grown up around me. I can honestly say I have loved people and tried my best to help make a positive difference in their lives.

I'm embarrassed about my frequent use of guilt trips and manipulation as I attempted to motivate people. I'm embarrassed over my tendency to try every gimmick, trick and strategy in the book. I'm embarrassed at how I've often sounded frantic, stressed, and full of strain as I represented the Kingdom of God.

I'm thankful and embarrassed, and I'm hopeful about my contribution in the body of Christ. I'm hopeful that I will continue to grow and change and be used by God. I hope to be a messenger of peace and rest in the church and in the world.

I hope to sound a little less churchified and a little more like Elijah saying, "God, you're the Hero of the story. Do what you do, I'm your servant."

CHAPTER 9 BIG IDEAS

"Do you want to stand out? Then step down. Be a servant. If you're content to simply be yourself, your life will count for plenty." (Matthew 23.11-12 MSG)

Church has never been perfect. We are stained and full of flaws, yet God continues to use us (which reminds us once again that He is the Hero of the story, not us).

The church gets a lot right. We also have a lot of things backwards.

If we're giving people guilt-trips, impossible religious standards that even the pastors and leaders aren't keeping up with, and a long list of tips on how to do more and be better, we have it backwards.

The Kingdom Message is one of peace and rest...

It announces that we have peace with God—not because of anything we've done, but because of what He has done for us.

It declares, "It is finished." God has done all the heavy lifting for us. We can rest in Him, knowing that He loves us perfectly and nothing will ever change that.

Often, our churchified selves depend more on upping the ante, increasing the intensity, straining and stressing to do more in order to make something happen... "Do more. Work harder. Try again. Climb the ladder."

Fruit is never the result of gimmicks, tricks, and strategies.

The real fruit and the best results always come from that quiet place of confidence in the Hero, where we have true peace and rest.

Fruitfulness follows peace and rest.

QUESTIONS
FOR INDIVIDUAL &/OR GROUP STUDY

1. What's the funniest thing you've ever seen or experienced in church life?

2. Why isn't the church more perfect?

3. Have you ever been amazed that God actually wants to use the flawed and imperfect you to accomplish His purposes?

4. Why is the churchified mantra, "Do more, work harder, try again, climb the ladder" destructive in God's Kingdom?

5. Why are we so attracted to gimmicks, tricks, and strategies?

6. What have you noticed about real fruit and the best results in your life?

You're the shepherd of my heart.
 —Johnny Cash (Shepherd of My Heart)

I am the Good Shepherd; I know my sheep and my sheep know me.
—Jesus (John 10.14 NIV)

10. SHEEP

When I was a kid, my mom had us memorize chapters of the Bible, verse by verse, each night at the dinner table. If you wanted dessert, you memorized that night's verse. Also, you couldn't leave the table until you had the verse memorized.

Sugar has always motivated me, so I was quick to learn the memory verses. There were four of us kids at the table, and I was usually the first or second one to quote the verse and get my dessert.

My dad, on the other hand, wasn't quite as fast. Many nights he would be the last one at the table, still trying to get the verse right, and really frustrated that he wasn't eating dessert yet.

One of the chapters we memorized was the 23rd Psalm.

Recently, I spent some time paraphrasing it because I wanted to be more conscious of its meaning and not just quote it from the New King James Version that I had memorized from years and years ago. Sometimes when you have something memorized, you stop thinking about the meaning and you just run on autopilot. I wanted to make myself think: what is God saying to me in these verses?

THE HERO OF MY STORY

Here's my paraphrase of the 23rd Psalm:

I have all the strength and supply I need.

I have peace.
And I have rest.

I'm headed in the right direction
because my Shepherd is guiding me.

Even when the way is clouded-over,
a dark valley that smells like death, threatening and
depressing—I am not afraid of anything.

I have God WITH me.
I am protected.
I am comforted.
I am refreshed.

I am honored and blessed—both in front of my friends
and those who don't like me.

Unlimited grace and unconditional love follow me
everywhere I go.

I am secure in my place, calm and confident.
I am home. I am family. This is where I belong.

All of this is not because of me. It's all because of Him...
My God, my Shepherd.
The Hero of my story.

SMELLS LIKE DEATH

One of the things I love most about the 23rd Psalm is that
it's not just an exercise in positive thinking; it's not about
living in denial of real challenges and difficulties.

These verses deal with the realities of life, the ups and
downs.

The Psalm takes us from lush pastures and peaceful streams to threatening skies and dark valleys that smell like death. It acknowledges the presence of enemies. And it reminds us that God is WITH us through it all.

This is a picture of real life...

The bright shining mountain tops of victory;
deep dark valleys of defeat.

Friends and fans singing praises;
antagonists and enemies ready to pounce.

Good days; bad days.

Strength; weakness.

Health; sickness.

Success; failure.

Joys; sorrows.

Birth; death.

Yes, through it all God is WITH us. The Shepherd never leaves our side. We make it, not because of our own strengths and abilities, but because of His faithfulness.

We are secure and confident, we have peace and rest, because there is a Hero to our story—our God, our Shepherd.

CHAPTER 10 BIG IDEAS

"I am the Good Shepherd; I know my sheep and my sheep know me." (John 10.14 NIV)

The 23rd Psalm is not just an exercise in positive thinking; it's not about living in denial of real challenges and difficulties.

These verses deal with the realities of life, the ups and downs.

Through it all God is WITH us.

The Shepherd never leaves our side. We make it, not because of our own strengths and abilities, but because of His faithfulness.

We are secure and confident, we have peace and rest, because there is a Hero to our story—our God, our Shepherd.

QUESTIONS
FOR INDIVIDUAL &/OR GROUP STUDY

1. What verses or sections of Scripture have you memorized? How has memorizing Scripture been helpful to you?

2. What is your favorite part of the 23rd Psalm? Why?

3. How do you keep Scripture that you have known for years fresh and alive for today?

4. How have you experienced God WITH you in the dark valleys of life?

5. What does God as the "Hero to our story" mean to you?

6. Have you written your own paraphrase of a passage of Scripture before? Will you accept the challenge of writing your own paraphrase of the 23rd Psalm this week?

Peace will come to me. I'm leaving bitterness behind.
This time I'm cleaning up my mind. There is no space for the
regrets. I will remember to forget.
  —Depeche Mode (Peace)

You, Lord, give perfect peace to those who keep their
purpose firm and put their trust in You.
  —Isaiah (Isaiah 26.3 GNT)

11. PEACEFUL

Near my home in Maple Valley, Washington, there is a trail that goes past Lake Wilderness and continues east for more than five miles. Over the past few years, I've enjoyed running on this trail by myself.

My favorite is to run the trail's full length. This takes about an hour, and another hour to return home. After about 35 minutes from my house, the trail leaves the populated area, goes into the woods and eventually spills into a wide-open field with a majestic view of Mt. Rainier. It's one of the most beautiful, peaceful places I know.

There's rarely anyone else out that far on the trail. The alone-time is recharging and feeds my soul. I honestly don't go out with a plan to "meet with God," but that's exactly what happens nearly every time.

Out there in the wilderness, there's no one else to talk to. It's just me and God.

I don't pray through an outline or 12-point plan, I just enjoy being aware of Him and being with Him. Sometimes I have something to say, but more often than not, I am just listening.

In the peace and quiet of my wilderness trail, I hear God whispering to me.

LETTING GO

Leaving the constant noise and activity of regular life for two hours on the trail into the beauty of creation as I become more fully aware of God's presence is life-giving, refreshing, calming, and settles me with peace.

For me, it is the 23rd Psalm enacted; resting in green pastures and being led beside peaceful streams by my Shepherd. It is peace and rest fully illustrated.

There is a "letting go" that happens on my trail, both figuratively and literally. Of course, I'm letting go of the hustle and bustle; I'm leaving all the advertisements, the clamoring for my attention, and the distractions behind. I also do a lot of sweating.

I've gotten into this habit of weighing myself before and after each run. It started because I was curious. I wanted to know how much weight was sweated out. The first time I weighed myself after one of these runs, I was shocked. I came home 3.4lbs lighter. That's so gross when you think about it. I sweat 54.4 ounces in two hours.

Quite literally, I am letting go of 54.4 ounces of sweat while on my run.

Often in life, letting go is the prerequisite for receiving something else.

I believe receiving the peace of God happens when we let go...

When we surrender.

When we put up the white flag.

When we drop our defenses and impenetrable facades.

When we stop being so competitive and get to the place where we don't have to win.

When we lay down our swords and weapons for battle.

CULTIVATE

I love the imagery of Isaiah 2.4 where it talks about the hammering of swords into farming tools. The picture is one of removing the edge of the blade and its purpose for battle in order to transform it into a tool for cultivating the ground. It's a description of letting go of violence in order to receive a better way of life.

Instead of destroying people and things, we cultivate. We plant things and watch them grow. Instead of arming ourselves to battle, we are equipping ourselves for peace.

This is the counter-cultural, subversive way of God's Kingdom.

In God's Kingdom, the strongest, loudest, and most powerful will not be able to force their way to the top. No. Instead, the greatest in the Kingdom is the servant of all.

Jesus didn't come to assert control and power over everyone. He came to serve, and to give His life as a peace offering. He is described as "The Prince of Peace" (Isaiah 9.6), not "The Aggressive Alpha Male."

God's act of reconciling us to Himself announces, "We're OK."

I love that. It's the ultimate statement of peace, "You and me, we're OK."

It's like the Australian saying, "No worries."

No harm, no foul.

I want to be more like this. I want to be known as someone who reconciles, who sends the message to those around me, "You and me, we're OK; no worries; no harm, no foul."

I want to be peaceful; full of peace, and as a result, peace-giving.

BIGGER WEAPONS

Yes, peace is the laying down of our swords—our instruments of aggression, power, control, and revenge (whether actual weapons or schemes or even just words).

Remember when Peter cut Malchus' ear off? Jesus rebuked him, telling him to put his sword down. Then He said, "Those who use the sword will die by the sword." (Mark 14.52 NLT).

Isn't that the truth? Someone will always have a bigger weapon than we do. We will always lose when we choose to abandon peace in favor of power and force.

Jesus put Malchus' ear back on and healed him. Talk about strange! Peter's desire to fight in that moment is completely understandable because it's the normal way we deal with attacks. You push me, I'll push you back. You show up with swords, I'll pull mine out and cut somebody's ear off.

But the way of the Kingdom is different. It's a little strange. It's definitely counterintuitive and countercultural. Jesus didn't resist arrest. Instead, He healed the arresting officer's ear.

Kingdom life isn't about swords, it's about peace.

Peace is better...

Peace is trusting that God's plan is greater than our understanding of what seems to be going on. Peace invites us to take a bigger view and consider God's work in our lives as it relates to eternity, not just today.

Peace is taking the Beatitude seriously, "Happy are those who work for peace; God will call them His children!" (Matthew 5.9 GNT).

Peace is concerned with MY PART. It isn't keeping score; it's not concerned about what others are doing wrong. It does everything possible to live at peace with everybody, even when they are doing the opposite. "Do everything possible on your part to live in peace with everybody." (Romans 12.18 GNT).

Peace is being content with life; it's being OK in our own skin, settled and all right with ourselves and the world.

Peace isn't about being good at competing; it's a state of being. It never interprets others losing as an opportunity for me to win.

Peace is recognizing, "I'm His kid, and that's all that really matters."

Peace is confidence in Him and His ability to turn anything around for the good. "We are confident that God is able to orchestrate everything to work toward something good and beautiful when we love Him and accept his invitation to live according to His plan." (Romans 8.28 TVB)

CHAPTER 11 BIG IDEAS

"You, Lord, give perfect peace to those who keep their purpose firm and put their trust in You." (Isaiah 26.3 GNT)

Often in life, letting go is the prerequisite for receiving something else.

Instead of destroying people and things, we cultivate. We plant things and watch them grow. Instead of arming ourselves to battle, we are equipping ourselves for peace.

In God's Kingdom, the strongest, loudest, and most powerful will not be able to force their way to the top. No. Instead, the greatest in the Kingdom is the servant of all.

Jesus didn't come to assert control and power over everyone. He came to serve, and to give His life as a peace offering. He is described as "The Prince of Peace" (Isaiah 9.6), not "The Aggressive Alpha Male."

God's act of reconciling us to Himself announces, "We're OK."

Someone will always have a bigger weapon than we do. We will always lose when we chose to abandon peace in favor of power and force.

Kingdom life isn't about swords, it's about peace.

QUESTIONS
FOR INDIVIDUAL &/OR GROUP STUDY

1. Where is the most peaceful place you know? What makes it so peaceful to you?

2. Where are you when you most frequently hear God whispering to you?

3. What do you need to let go of in order to receive the peace that God has for you?

4. How is Kingdom of God peace counter-cultural and subversive?

5. How have you experienced the loss of peace when you chose the way of power and force?

6. God reconciles people to Himself. He also enlists His people in the work of reconciling others (2 Corinthians 5.18-19). In what ways have you been used by God to reconcile others to Him?

Carry on, my wayward son. For there'll be peace when you are done. Lay your weary head to rest, don't you cry no more.
—Kansas (Carry On Wayward Son)

I find rest in God; only He gives me hope.
He is my rock and my salvation. He is my defender.
—David (Psalm 62.5-6 NCV)

12. RESTFUL

My wife and I agree...

Our number one piece of marriage advice - go on (more) vacations together!

I'm really not much of a counselor and I don't do marriage counseling. My advice isn't very sophisticated—I say the same things to everyone:

Be nice to each other. Laugh more together. Don't just talk about your problems all the time, that's not healthy. If you keep picking a scab, it will never have a chance to heal. Make sure you're having fun together.

Go on dates. Do things you enjoy together. Get a babysitter. Stop making excuses. Date each other.

Take a vacation with your spouse. Regularly. More.

That's all I got. But hey, it works for my marriage!

Shari and I are constantly amazed at how few married couples actually get away together.

Vacations remind us that we enjoy being together. They force us to stop thinking about work and start having conversations about shared interests. These times away build our marriage and strengthen our relationship.

Big vacations, small vacations; local trips and travels around the world—we think every couple needs to budget, save, and plan for VACATIONS.

We've always budgeted for vacations. And we've been pretty blessed. Sure, there have been times where "vacation" meant staying at a relative's house or even staying at home and hitting up a few local favorite spots while taking a few days off work. But we've also been around the world together.

Last year, Shari noticed advertisements for package deals to Iceland. Half-joking, she asked me if I wanted to go (she thought I would instantly turn her down and tell her to only look for deals in warm-weather locations). To her surprise, I said, "Yes. Let's go! I want you to take me there for my birthday."

Within a few days, we booked the trip. It was absolutely amazing. The place is like an Instagramer's wildest dream. I loved it, and I can't wait to go back.

SELAH

One of the great things about vacations is that they create a pause, or break, from the usual.

God wants us to pause.

"Be still, and know that I am God!" (Psalm 46.10 NLT).

Jesus not only modeled His own times of rest and solitude, but He made sure the disciples rested too. "Then, because so many people were coming and going that they did not even have a chance to eat, He said to them, 'Come with me by yourselves to a quiet place and get some rest.'" (Mark 6.31 NIV).

Sometimes we believe we can't afford to rest because the demands are too high and our work is so significant. Funny... what we have to do doesn't come anywhere close to what

Jesus had to do, and yet He still managed to prioritize regular times of rest and getting away from it all. Look, if Jesus could make time to pause and rest, so can we.

I've grown to love the word "Selah." I appreciate and enjoy Selah. And I want more Selah in my life.

In the Psalms, Selah indicates a musical interlude. It's announcing that it's time for a break from the lyrics. Just music, no words. Take a breather. Give your brain a chance to catch up. Process what you've heard.

The Amplified Bible interprets Selah as, "Pause and think..."

Resting allows us to think, process, consider, reflect, evaluate, and catch up. Rest is Selah. It's an interlude, a necessary break. It helps you to appreciate what you've just been through, and it makes you look forward to what's ahead.

Rest is a pause.

Rest is a break from the usual.

Rest is easy. It's not exerting or straining.

Rest is keeping a safe distance from all of the noise.

Rest is a reminder: we're not that important. Life continues on without us.

Rest is learning to enjoy not working.

Rest is in the moment, in the flow.

Rest is telling urgency "no."

Rest is perspective.

Rest is life-giving.

Rest is recharging.

Rest is stillness.

Rest is quiet.

Rest is calm.

I'll be honest: sometimes rest is work. You know what I mean? Unplugging from the phone and social media and all the usual outlets of communication can be like going through withdrawals. It's pretty embarrassing.

I've found the more frequently I rest, the better I get at it. It's easier that way. And when times of unplugging and getting away from it all are fewer and farther between, it's always more difficult to adjust.

This thought brings me back to something I said earlier: Go on more vacations! There is Someone who wants to go with you...

"My presence will travel with you, and I will give you rest." (Exodus 33.14 VOICE)

CHAPTER 12 BIG IDEAS

"I find rest in God; only He gives me hope. He is my rock and my salvation. He is my defender." (Psalm 62.5-6 NCV)

God wants us to pause. "Be still, and know that I am God!" (Psalm 46.10 NLT).

Jesus not only modeled His own times of rest and solitude, but He made sure the disciples rested too. "Then, because so many people were coming and going that they did not even have a chance to eat, He said to them, 'Come with me by yourselves to a quiet place and get some rest.'" (Mark 6.31 NIV).

Sometimes we believe we can't afford to rest because the demands are too high and our work is so significant. Funny... what we have to do doesn't come anywhere close to what Jesus had to do, and yet He still managed to prioritize regular times of rest and getting away from it all. If Jesus could make time to pause and rest, so can we.

I've grown to love the word "Selah." I appreciate and enjoy Selah. And I want more Selah in my life.

Resting allows us to think, process, consider, reflect, evaluate, and catch up. Rest is Selah. It's an interlude, a necessary break. It helps you to appreciate what you've just been through, and it makes you look forward to what's ahead.

I'll be honest: sometimes rest is work. You know what I mean?

QUESTIONS
FOR INDIVIDUAL &/OR GROUP STUDY

1. What is one vacation you've been on that you think everyone should experience?

2. Where is a place you haven't been to yet but really want to go someday?

3. What does "Selah" mean to you? When are the times you most frequently experience Selah?

4. What wonderful things does rest provide for you?

5. How is rest sometimes work (or like a chore) for you?

6. How can rest become natural, easy, and enjoyable in our lives?

Stop putting your conscience on cease and bring about some type of peace. Not only in your heart, but also in your mind—it will benefit all mankind.
—Queen Latifah (Evil That Men Do)

Praise the Lord, my soul, and forget not all His benefits...
—David (Psalm 103.2 NIV)

13. BENEFITS

I'm a loyal Starbucks customer—have been for years. You could say I'm a big fan. I'm not an evangelist; I'm not trying to convert anyone over to Starbucks. I just want it, every day of my life.

My wife and I disagree on this issue. She is not a Starbucks fan. She prefers coffee that tastes more like chocolate and comes from a store that sells lots of chocolate. She has zero interest in Starbucks. When she does end up getting something from Starbucks, she complains that it tastes like Starbucks.

Being a regular Starbucks customer has its benefits. I have "my" Starbucks, the one closest to my house—the one I frequent the most. They know my name there. They know what I do for a living. They know what I drink. And when the store is busy and the line is long, they start on my drink before I even get to the register.

If I'm away on a trip and don't come in for several days, they miss me (or at least they act like they do... either way, I appreciate it).

And I get free drinks too. I'm not completely sure how it all works, but I think it has something to do with the volume of coffee I've been purchasing.

Starbucks gives me free music through their iPhone app. They send me e-mails about new products and special deals coming up.

The bottom line? When you're a regular at Starbucks, there are benefits.

The same is true with peace and rest.

When we embrace God's gift of peace and rest in our lives, there are benefits that follow us everywhere we go.

Some benefits of peace...

Peace makes us secure.

Peace settles our spirits.

Peace empowers us to forgive.

Peace reminds us that we are forgiven.

Peace makes our homes a refuge, a safe place.

Peace builds bridges and brings people together.

Peace reminds us that we are loved, the way we are, right now.

Peace allows us to say with conviction, "This battle is not mine to fight."

Peace helps us see what we have in common with one another.

Peace prevents us from being paranoid.

Peace produces strength and stability.

Peace allows us to sleep at night.

Peace brings health.

And some benefits of rest…

Rest rejuvenates.

Rest clarifies our focus.

Rest increases our strength.

Rest helps us to dream again.

Rest makes us look and feel better.

Rest makes space and time for healing.

Rest gives us courage for new challenges.

Rest causes us to forget what we were so angry about.

Rest allows us to see and hear what we've been missing.

Rest helps to close the chapter and sets the stage for the next one to be written.

GET BOTH

Once, on a trip to Swaziland, I met a maintenance man who worked at the Bible College there. He was a nice guy, but there was something about him that struck me as odd. He was wearing a bright red construction hat on his head and flip flops on his feet. The combination didn't make sense to me. I guess when it really comes down to it, you can lose your feet, but you can't lose your head and make it out alive. But still, if you feel the need to protect your head, wouldn't you at least do something to protect your feet?

Flip flops and a construction hat? That's just silly. He needed some good work boots to go along with that hat.

Peace and rest are best when present together in our lives. In fact, they don't work when they're separated from each other.

When we have peace and rest, we actually begin to like ourselves. We're more content, creative, and productive.

And you know what?

When we have peace and rest the people around us are grateful too—they feel better about us and like us a lot more than our peaceless, restless selves.

I'm not a Starbucks evangelist. I don't really care where you get your coffee or if you even like coffee. I am, however, a Kingdom of God evangelist...

I want everyone to experience the peace and rest that comes from our loving Father.

The benefits are out of this world.

And our world really needs 'em.

CHAPTER 13 BIG IDEAS

"Praise the Lord, my soul, and forget not all His benefits..." (Psalm 103.2 NIV)

When we embrace God's gift of peace and rest in our lives, there are benefits that follow us everywhere we go.

Peace and rest are best when present together in our lives. In fact, they don't work when they're separated from each other.

When we have peace and rest, we actually begin to like ourselves. We're more content, creative, and productive.

When we have peace and rest the people around us are grateful too—they feel better about us and like us a lot more than our peaceless, restless selves.

I want everyone to experience the peace and rest that comes from our loving Father. The benefits are out of this world, and our world really needs 'em.

QUESTIONS
FOR INDIVIDUAL &/OR GROUP STUDY

1. Where are you a loyal customer who enjoys the benefits that go along with being a regular there? What are some of the benefits?

2. What are some of the benefits of peace you see in your life?

3. What are some of the benefits of rest you see in your life?

4. Have you experienced liking yourself more when you have enough peace and rest?

5. When are you most content, creative, or productive?

6. When we (Kingdom of God people) are functioning with the peace and rest He provides, how does the world around us benefit?

We just need some sleep to dream away these fears. We just need some time to clear our crowded minds.
—Sleeping At Last (Slowly Now)

Tuck me in. I need to sleep now, I need to dream how I used to dream. Look me in the face now. Help me believe how I used to believe.
—Echo and the Bunnymen (In The Margins)

They got into a boat and started out. As they sailed across, Jesus settled down for a nap.
(Luke 8.22-23 NLT)

14. NAP

I like big naps, I cannot lie.

Actually, I like all kinds of naps. It's probably a sign of my old age. Sometimes on my day off I get up in the morning, have some coffee and breakfast, then go right back upstairs for a nap. It's great. You should try it sometime.

There are actually six locations around our house where I enjoy napping. I consider myself to be somewhat of a napping connoisseur. The only nap I don't like is the one that accidentally turns into sleeping all night long.

My daughter does not share my passion for napping. I've never heard Ashah say, "I could really use a nap." In fact, she always denies that she needs one. She avoids naps like they're some kind of highly contagious disease.

When she was younger, you could see the inevitable crash and burn happen right before your eyes when she was tired. Her mood would take a sudden nosedive, and our precious little girl turned into some kind of demon-child.

No amount of reasoning or consoling would turn it around. All we could do was make her take a nap and ride out the storm...

She would resist. Things would get worse. She would say terrible things. We questioned our parenting qualifications. Then, at the peak of the storm, Ashah would finally succumb to sleep—that full-fledged, sweaty hair and puffy lips, sleep through anything for hours kind-of-nap.

Watching her sleep, we knew that our diagnosis was correct: she needed a nap. As much as she denied it, it was exactly what she needed.

THE PROPHET CRASHES AND BURNS

When it comes to peace and rest, I think we sometimes act like children denying the need for a nap and resisting with all our might until we finally break. We have endless excuses, reasons why our strain and stress is so absolutely necessary.

The suggestion that we might need more peace and rest in our lives makes us defensive and irritable. And sometimes, it's not until we hit the peak of the storm that we finally succumb...

Admitting that we need help. Supernatural intervention. Peace that only God can give. Rest that restores our soul.

The prophet Elijah did this very thing.

He was an important "man of God." He had a successful ministry. He spoke, and people listened. And perhaps he momentarily forgot who the Hero really was.

While in a flurry of activity doing "big things" for God, he had a meltdown...

Elijah crashed and burned. His mood took a sudden nosedive. He went from man of God to demon-child overnight. Elijah was carrying the weight of the world on his shoulders, which can be both intoxicating and addictive. He started to believe...

I'm working so hard, doing so much—I'm irreplaceable.

I'm the only one who sees, understands, and gets it.

Without me, everything will fall apart.

Nobody else cares as much as I do.

The frenzied pace of trying to be the solution, answer man, and super-achiever quickly spun out of control. Elijah was suddenly toxic, full of strain and stress.

The result?

Anger

Frustration

Depression

Excuses

Blame

Sometimes, we need to be reminded that the world doesn't actually rest on our shoulders and that we aren't the only ones who see, understand, and get it. There is still time for naps, and we should probably take one.

Elijah had to learn this lesson. He desperately needed some peace and rest. He had become delusional, intoxicated from drinking his own Kool-Aid, and was addicted to carrying the weight of the world on his shoulders.

He believed he was the only one. The hope of the world. The hero of the story.

The funny thing is, the Bible tells us there were 7,000 others just like him (1 Kings 19.18 and Romans 11.3-4). Nope, Elijah wasn't The One. He was 1 of 7,000.

Elijah had become self-absorbed and self-important. He was working alone and experiencing burnout. The prophet was frustrated, angry, and depressed.

God's solution?

He had Elijah take a rest from working, have several naps, and eat properly. And after that, God directed Elijah to recruit someone younger to begin working with him.

Interesting, isn't it? Even prophets need naptime.

It's a great reminder for all of us who are doing "big things." We all need breaks, naps, healthy food, and some young people around us to invest in.

We need, whether we're willing to admit it or not, more peace and rest.

CHAPTER 14 BIG IDEAS

When it comes to peace and rest, we sometimes act like children denying the need for a nap and resisting with all our might until we finally break. We have endless excuses, reasons why our strain and stress is so absolutely necessary.

The suggestion that we might need more peace and rest in our lives makes us defensive and irritable. And sometimes, it's not until we hit the peak of the storm that we finally succumb... Admitting that we need help. Supernatural intervention. Peace that only God can give. Rest that restores our soul.

Sometimes, we need to be reminded that the world doesn't actually rest on our shoulders and that we aren't the only ones who see, understand, and get it. There is still time for naps, and we should probably take one.

It's a great reminder for all of us who are doing "big things." We all need breaks, naps, healthy food, and some young people around us to invest in.

We need, whether we're willing to admit it or not, more peace and rest.

QUESTIONS
FOR INDIVIDUAL &/OR GROUP STUDY

1. What is your favorite kind of nap?

2. How does eating right (or wrong) affect your mood?

3. Have you ever been so caught up doing big and important things that you didn't even realize how miserable and annoying you were?

4. Do you sometimes behave as if the world does rest on your shoulders? Why?

5. Are regular times of rest and healthy eating spiritual activities? Explain.

6. Why do we need younger people around us?

I sometimes get worried and I wonder why I worry, 'cause I know that I will make it through the storm.
—Mary J Blige (Keep Your Head)

Into this house we're born, into this world we're thrown. Like a dog without a bone, an actor out on loan. Riders on the storm.
—The Doors (Riders on the Storm)

And the rain descended, the floods came, and the winds blew and beat on that house; and it did not fall, for it was founded on the rock.
 —Jesus (Matthew 7.25 NKJV)

15. STORM

While staying in Italy recently, my family experienced some stormy Italian weather. We were leaving a small hilltop café and returning to our rented countryside cottage. The owner of the cottage, a 70+ year-old British lady, was driving. Just as we walked out the door of the café, rain started coming down in torrents, with lightening flashing across the sky and huge thunder booms following almost immediately. Then came the hail.

As we packed into Phyllis' car (a tiny 1980's Italian Fiat), we brought a lot of moisture along with us. Moisture and warm bodies in a tiny car from the 1980's means fogged-up windows that are nearly impossible to cure.

I thought maybe Phyllis would just pull the car over and wait...

Wait for the blinding hail to stop.
Wait for the windows to defrost and clear up.
Wait for safe driving conditions.

But not Phyllis. She seemed to be in a hurry to get us home. Maybe there was something on TV starting in five minutes that she didn't want to miss seeing. I don't know what the hurry was, but one thing was clear: Phyllis was on a mission to get us home.

She drove, and I couldn't see where. I was in the passenger seat, so I grabbed a rag and started wiping down the windshield. This provided about three seconds of 18% visibility before the window clouded completely over again. And Phyllis drove on.

I think she was driving, as they say, "by Braille."

We were obviously off the road a few times, which seemed rather treacherous considering the winding hilltop road we were travelling on. Hail pelted the car. The thunder and lighting combos seemed to be getting closer.

In the middle of our blind drive through the storm, there was a sudden bright white flash and loud crack of thunder all at the same time. I could hear my wife in the back seat asking if we'd been hit. My daughter was saying something about smelling smoke.

Phyllis, in her perfect Julie Andrews-sounding British accent, said, "Oh my, I DO NOT like this lightening." And she continued to drive.

The 2.5 kilometer drive took 15 minutes in the storm. Finally, we arrived safe and sound (minus a few hail injuries and smelling like smoke) at Casa Alloro.

While I wasn't really afraid for our lives during this Italian storm, I was certain that what we were experiencing would be a life memory—one of those, "Remember when that storm hit and we were riding in Phyllis' Fiat..." kind of stories.

STRANGE THEOLOGIES

Storms, whether literal or figurative, often cause us to lose sight of the future. They make us wonder if we are going to make it or not. And perhaps even more dangerous than the actual storm happening is the storm of fear that rises in our hearts.

People have a tendency to develop strange theologies about storms. Some see them as the judgment of God because of the wickedness of a particular group of people, a city, or even nation. It seems like every time there's a terrible tragedy somewhere in the world, the prophets of doom and gloom start making media appearances talking about God's judgment.

I think it's just plain stupid.

While on a ministry tour with Jesus, the disciples didn't like how a particular village treated Jesus. James and John (AKA: The Thunder Brothers) wanted quick and decisive judgment. They asked Jesus if they should call down a tornado of fire from heaven to burn up the offensive town.

But Jesus said, "You do not know what manner of spirit you are of. For the Son of Man did not come to destroy men's lives but to save them." (Luke 9.55-56 NKJV).

Basically, Jesus was saying, "If you think that sounds like me, you're incredibly confused. I came to save people, not send storms of judgment on them."

Somehow, the doom and gloom prophets think what they're saying sounds like God, but they are really confused. I think they might have skipped some key parts of their Bible reading plans—like this one: "For God chose to save us through our Lord Jesus Christ, not to pour out His anger on us." (1 Thessalonians 5.9 NLT).

There's a huge book in the Bible about one man, Job, and his family who went through a horrific storm, experiencing pain, loss, and great suffering. Job's friends were convinced his storm was the result of some secret sin in his life. If you've read the story, you know they were completely wrong.

The Bible says, "He has set a day for judging the world with His justice by the Man He has appointed..." (Acts 17.31 NLT). There you have it. He will judge the world with justice by the man (Jesus) He has appointed. Until Jesus comes again, we need to stop focusing on judgment and get busy announcing the Good News of the Kingdom of God, the Good News that declares:

"We have been given peace with God; we are reconciled to Him through the sacrifice of Jesus on the cross."

God has given us rest. Our sins have all been forgiven. We are loved and accepted by Him, therefore we can rest in His work that says, "It is finished."

Storms aren't a sign of God's judgment. They are part of life. Jesus said, "I have told you these things so that you will be whole and at peace. In this world, you will be plagued with times of trouble, but you need not fear; I have triumphed over this corrupt world order." (John 16.33 VOICE)

Yes, storms will come and storms will go, but God wants us to have peace before, during, all the way through, and after every storm we face.

SLEEPING ON A BOAT IN A STORM

In one of my favorite stories about Jesus, He has a nap while taking a boat trip across the lake with His disciples. I love this! I'm so thankful the Bible gave us this little detail...

Jesus likes naps, just like I do.

I've often wondered if perhaps Jesus had gotten a little queasy while riding on the boat. They probably didn't have Dramamine back then. Whenever I get car sick or seasick, I always lie down and try to sleep through it. Someday, I'm going to ask Jesus about that.

Whether He was seasick or not, we don't know. What we do know, is that He was out for the count. One of those sweaty hair, puffy lips, able to sleep through anything kind-of-naps.

"But soon a fierce storm came up. High waves were breaking into the boat, and it began to fill with water." (Mark 4.37 NLT)

And what was Jesus doing?

Catching some Z's. Probably having a great dream about eating pita chips and hummus or something like that.

"Jesus was sleeping at the back of the boat with His head on a cushion." (Mark 4.38 NLT) All the movement, noise, and even water sloshing around His body didn't wake Him up. He was having a serious nap.

Finally, the disciples lost their cool and were in panic mode. "The disciples woke Him up, shouting, 'Teacher, don't you care that we're going to drown?'" (Mark 4.38 NLT).

The disciples were stressed out. They'd been straining with all their might to save themselves, and it wasn't working. Not knowing what else to do, they woke Jesus up and lodged a complaint...

"You don't care."

The truth is, Jesus did care. He was operating at a whole different level of peace and rest though, and His disciples didn't know how to interpret that. To them, it just looked like Jesus was being all nonchalant about their storm.

It would have made them feel better if Jesus had freaked-out too; stressing and straining right along with them. But having someone stress and strain with us isn't the same as having The Hero bring peace to our storm. We don't need another freak-out partner; we need Someone with authority to calmly speak to the wind and the waves.

"Jesus stood up and commanded the wind, 'Be quiet!' and He said to the waves, 'Be still!' The wind died down, and there was a great calm." (Mark 4.39 GNT)

See what Jesus does fresh out of a nap? He hadn't even gotten His coffee yet.

But seriously, what an incredible Hero we have. Afraid of nothing. Never shaken. Doesn't stress or strain. He speaks calmly and with authority. He's the Prince of Peace. He is God who takes naps and knows how to rest.

GENTLE WHISPER OF THE HERO

He continues to speak to our storms today. "Be quiet. Be still."

The storms die down, and there is a great calm.

I believe He is speaking those same words, "Be quiet; be still," not just to our storms, but to our hearts as well. He wants us to experience the peace and rest that He gives even while we're hurting, struggling, and in the middle of our greatest storms.

A few years ago, my mom went into the hospital and the doctors weren't sure exactly what was going on, but they knew her kidneys had failed. I was at the hospital every day, not knowing if my mom was going to make it or not.

To be honest, I hated the uncertainty. I wanted answers. Each time I drove away from the hospital, I broke down and cried—wondering if I'd just had my last visit with my mom.

Eventually, the diagnosis came. We had answers...

They found that she had multiple myeloma, a cancer of the blood. The cancer was the cause of her kidney failure. She would need to be on dialysis three times a week and would begin an ongoing cycle of chemo.

This type of cancer is incurable. Treatments simply help keep the cancer at bay for a while and extend life a few more years.

In my family, this has been a storm. We didn't choose it. Nobody did anything to deserve it. Storms, like this one, just happen in life.

I'm not going to say it's been easy. If there was another option or way out, we'd choose it. But here we are, in this storm...

And we're experiencing the peace and rest that God provides.

This storm has been the hardest on my mom. To say she's been experiencing trouble, pain, and difficulty would be an understatement. And yet, I've never seen my mom more full of joy than she is now. She has received the wonderful peace and rest of God in the middle of her storm, and the fruit of it is evident in her life.

Through all the doctor appointments, chemo treatments, surgeries, setbacks, long days at dialysis, and struggles of being a cancer patient, my mom is hearing the gentle whisper of The Hero, saying, "Be quiet; be still. Don't worry about a thing, I am your source of peace and rest."

CHAPTER 15 BIG IDEAS

"And the rain descended, the floods came, and the winds blew and beat on that house; and it did not fall, for it was founded on the rock." (Matthew 7.25 NKJV)

Storms, whether literal or figurative, often cause us to lose sight of the future. They make us wonder if we are going to make it or not. And perhaps even more dangerous than the actual storm happening is the storm of fear that rises in our hearts.

Storms aren't a sign of God's judgment. They are part of life.

Storms will come and storms will go, but God wants us to have peace before, during, all the way through, and after every storm we face.

Having someone stress and strain with us isn't the same as having The Hero bring peace to our storm. We don't need another freak-out partner; we need Someone with authority to calmly speak to the wind and the waves.

He is speaking those same words, "Be quiet; be still," not just to our storms, but to our hearts as well. He wants us to experience the peace and rest that He gives even while we're hurting, struggling, and in the middle of our greatest storms.

QUESTIONS
FOR INDIVIDUAL &/OR GROUP STUDY

1. What's the craziest weather you have ever experienced? Were you scared for your life? Why?

2. Have you ever had an out-of-control storm of fear rise up in your heart? What was happening? How did you survive the storm?

3. In what ways are you beginning to realize that storms are just part of life?

4. Does it ever bother you when you're freaking out about something and your friends or family appear to be calm and not very concerned?

5. When freaking out, do you tend to gravitate toward people who are also freaking out, or those who are calm and peaceful? Why?

6. How have you sensed the whisper of God saying, "Be quiet, be still" while hurting, struggling, or in the middle of a great storm?

People here are friendly and content. People here are colorful and bright. The flowers often bloom at night.
—REM (The Flowers of Guatemala)

I have learned in whatever state I am, to be content: I know how to be abased, and I know how to abound. Everywhere and in all things I have learned both to be full and to be hungry, both to abound and to suffer need.
—Paul (Philippians 4.11-12 NKJV)

16. BE

My parents are the most frugal people I know. Just recently, my dad (who has been retired since he turned 50, some 15+ years ago) was telling me how they have soooooo much money now because they're finally old enough to collect Social Security.

He and my mom are getting something like $1,600 a month from Social Security – which is more than they've been living off of for the past 15 years. Do you see what I mean? They have a simple, frugal lifestyle.

Of course, for many years, my dad worked at a good job and brought home a lot more money each month than his Social Security check. My parents know how to be wealthy and they know how to be poor. They've done it very well.

Paul the apostle wrote a letter from prison and said, "I have learned in whatever state I am, to be content: I know how to be abased, and I know how to abound. Everywhere and in all things I have learned both to be full and to be hungry, both to abound and to suffer need. I can do all things through Christ who strengthens me." (Philippians 4.11-13 NKJV)

I think there's a valuable lesson in those words...

"I know how to be."

I know how to be poor. I know how to be rich.

I know how to be anonymous. I know how to be somebody.

I know how to be quiet. I know how to project my voice so others can hear.

I know how to be the back seat guy. I know how to be the take charge guy.

I know how to be subtle. I know how to be obvious.

I know how to be without. I know how to be well-off.

I know how to be still. I know how to be active.

I know how to be sad. I know how to laugh.

I know how to be right. I know how to be wrong.

Sometimes, we only know how to be on one side, the "good" side, of the list. When we find ourselves on the other side, we become unsettled, uncomfortable, and full of stress and strain.

When Paul wrote the "I know how to be..." verse, he was on the other side of the list. He was in prison. He was not living in the best conditions, yet he had peace and rest.

Paul was comfortable in his own skin. He was OK with his lot in life. He was content. His secret? Jesus gave him the strength "to be" whatever the circumstances demanded.

THE RULES CHANGED

When I transitioned from being a youth pastor to a lead pastor of a church, I had to re-learn "how to be." Honestly, it proved to be a more difficult transition than I had expected. I went from loving my job, to wondering if I had made the biggest mistake of my life.

The circumstances were different. "How to be" a youth pastor isn't the same as "how to be" a lead pastor. The rules had changed.

Being a youth pastor wasn't very stressful. I didn't worry much about budgets—the church gave me a certain amount of money each year for the youth ministry, and I spent it.

Students admired me. They looked up to me. They wanted to be like me.

Young people are fun. They're flexible and quick to adapt. Leading change in a youth ministry is no sweat. They respond to vision and are easily inspired.

In a few days, I went from being a loved and admired leader of young people, to the young pastor who was ruining the church for people who used to like it before I showed up. Nobody was looking up to me anymore. I was getting more of a look of suspicion from people. Flexible and quick to adapt? Not a chance. Easily inspired? No, but some of them were wishing I could be easily fired.

Basically, I had to re-learn "how to be." The circumstances were different now. The old rules (the ones I had grown to love) didn't apply anymore and there was a new set of rules to learn through trial and error.

Thankfully, Jesus was my source of strength. It wasn't an easy transition, but I've made it, and I'm actually comfortable in my own skin. I'm OK with my lot in life. I'm content. And that's putting it conservatively. I've grown to love my role and the unique challenges that it brings. I'm having fun now - learning "how to be" a lead pastor.

WHEN THINGS CHANGE

Sometimes we get to choose the change in circumstances for ourselves. When we do, we're typically feeling more up for the adventure and challenge, knowing this choice means the old rules don't apply anymore and we'll have to re-learn "how to be."

We choose to get married. There are new rules. We learn how to be married.

We choose a new job. There are new rules. We learn how to be successful there.

We choose to lose weight. There are new rules. We learn how to be sugar free.

I've often thought it was funny watching people leave the church because they don't like how things have changed and they don't want to adapt to the changes.

So they go to a new church, where they have to change and adapt.

The new church has its way of doing things. There is change everywhere. Now at their new church, they have to park in a different place, sit in a different chair, meet new people, learn new ways of doing things, and get used to a new pastor.

They left because they don't like how things have changed and don't want to adapt to the changes, so they went somewhere that will require total change and adaptation.

See what I mean? It's funny.

But here's why they do it: because it's always easier to adapt and change when we are the ones choosing the new set of circumstances.

It's more difficult to be OK with change and make the necessary adjustments when the circumstances have been changed without our consent.

And while there are many circumstances in life that we get to choose, there are just as many (if not more) that we do not.

This is why we need strength from Jesus—so that in all circumstances, we know how to be...

Content

Full of peace

At rest

Up for the challenge

Alive, fully present, embracing this moment and all that it requires.

In the Amplified Bible where Paul is talking about knowing "how to be" because of the strength he receives from Christ, it adds this little phrase, "I am ready for anything."

What a great way to be.

CHAPTER 16 BIG IDEAS

"I have learned in whatever state I am, to be content: I know how to be abased, and I know how to abound. Everywhere and in all things I have learned both to be full and to be hungry, both to abound and to suffer need." (Philippians 4.11-12 NKJV)

Sometimes, we only know how to be on one side (the right side) of the list. When we find ourselves on the other side, we become unsettled, uncomfortable, and full of stress and strain.

It's always easier to adapt and change when we are the ones choosing the new set of circumstances.

It's more difficult to be OK with change and make the necessary adjustments when the circumstances have been changed without our consent.

While there are many circumstances in life that we get to choose, there are just as many (if not more) that we do not.

This is why we need strength from Jesus—so that in all circumstances, we know how to be...

QUESTIONS
FOR INDIVIDUAL &/OR GROUP STUDY

1. Have you been poor? Have you been well-off? How'd you do at being poor? How'd you do at being rich?

2. What is something you feel proficient in knowing "how to be?"

3. What is something you wish you knew better "how to be?"

4. When was a time in your life that the rules and circumstances changed because of your choosing? How did you feel? How well did you adapt?

5. When was a time in your life that the rules and circumstances changed without your choosing? How did you feel? How well did you adapt?

6. How have you experienced the strength Jesus provides when going through challenging experiences or circumstances, empowering you "to be" whatever the situation demanded?

Oh, I have only just discovered who I am and where I'm coming from. If you could see me now...
—Cartel (See Me Now)

I was so foolish and ignorant... yet I still belong to You.
—David (Psalm 72.22-23)

17. BELONG

Most of us spend years of our lives doing our best to fit in. We're like chameleons, changing our look to blend in with the surroundings.

Looking back, it makes me smile when I think about all the various characters I tried to play (it also makes me smile because I had hair back then).

I wanted to be Steve Largent so I started playing football. Unfortunately, I broke a finger playing football with some guys from church on a Sunday afternoon. The finger needed surgery and I had pins holding the fragments of bone together. My hopes of being the star wide receiver that year were dashed.

I wanted to be Tony Hawk so I bought a skateboard. Since I'd recently had surgery on my hand and had this metal brace holding my finger in the right position, I figured I could use my feet and legs to become a great skateboarder. Unfortunately, I wasn't very good. OK, I was terrible. I fell off my skateboard and landed on my hand with the surgically-repaired finger. The metal brace bent the wrong direction and all the stitches popped out. I had to go get another x-ray and stitched back up again. Then my mom took my skateboard away. Hopes were dashed again.

I wanted to be Billy Idol so I bleached my hair platinum and bought an electric guitar. I learned to play three chords, which someone told me is all you need to play punk rock music. After a few months, I was so sick and tired of those three chords that I started listening to Sir-Mix-a-Lot. Hey, maybe I could become a rap star...

I wanted to be Andy Warhol so I started painting. I was actually pretty good at this and even got an art scholarship. But I was uncertain about life as an artist and had this growing sense that God wanted to do something different with my life, so I ended up using the art scholarship to go to Bible college instead.

Through all these phases, I was searching for my fit. I was working to blend in, changing my look and doing my best to appear natural in these various surroundings.

And I was never settled. There was a void of security and confidence. It was a time of unrest and I didn't have peace about who I was. I wasn't comfortable in my own skin.

Maybe you can relate.

ONE DAY YOU'RE IN, AND THE NEXT DAY YOU'RE OUT

It's fun to look through old photos and see the various phases we went through...

The hair, the fashion, the friends, the hobbies, the passions, and the politics.

It's interesting how we can have the right "uniform," be saying all the right things, be surrounded by all the right people, and still feel that sense of unrest and lack of peace. As much as we try to fit in, we find ourselves still questioning, "Do I really fit here?"

We suspect we could get voted out. We worry that someone important in our group doesn't really approve of us. We're painfully aware of our own ability to mess things up for ourselves. We fear rejection and failure...

Because "fitting in" is always a moving target. It's not a once-and-then-done proposition. As Heidi Klum says on her reality TV show Project Runway, "In fashion, one day you're in, and the next day you're out." It sounds snotty, mean, and judgmental. And it's true.

What's worse is that we know it's true, not just for fashion, but for everything else too. Take the word "fashion" out of her sentence and replace it with "music" or "sports" or "popularity" or "business." It's still true.

One day you're in and the next day you're out.

Fitting in is elusive.

Even when you do, you're worried about what's next.

BELONGING IS BETTER

God doesn't want us to spend our lives trying to fit in. Instead, He offers something radically different: the right to belong.

"But to all who believed Him and accepted Him, He gave the right to become the children of God." (John 1.12 NLT)

"I was so foolish and ignorant... yet I still belong to You." (Psalm 73.22-23 NLT)

"So now there is no condemnation for those who belong to Christ Jesus. And because you belong to Him, the power of the life-giving Spirit has freed you from the power of sin that leads to death." (Romans 8.1-2 NLT)

That's right. God says, "You belong."

It's not about fitting in, it's about belonging. We are His children, His family. We belong.

This isn't a moving target like fitting in. It's sure and secure. Nothing will change this.

"And I am convinced that nothing can ever separate us from God's love... neither our fears for today nor our worries about tomorrow—not even the powers of hell can separate us from God's love. No power in the sky above or in the earth below—indeed, nothing in all creation will ever be able to separate us from the love of God that is revealed in Christ Jesus our Lord." (Romans 8.38-39 NLT)

Belonging gives us peace and rest in a way that fitting in never can.

I belong to my family. I belong when I'm behaving and when I'm misbehaving. I belong when I'm successful and when I'm failing. I belong when I make my family proud and when I make them sad. I belong, simply because I am family.

I don't have to do anything to fit in with my family. I already belong.

I'm pretty sure I'm the only one in my family who loves rap music. My wife listens to super mellow music (I'm not really sure what it is). My daughter listens to music made for middle-school girls. My sister listens to country music. My other sister listens to classical. My parents listen to the oldies.

We all listen to different stuff, and nobody has to feel insecure about their place in the family—because we're not trying to fit in; we belong.

In God's Kingdom, we belong—which is so much better than fitting in.

What an amazing place of peace and rest...

Where we belong.

Here, we are secure and confident. We know who we really are.

We are settled, and comfortable in our own skin. We are OK with ourselves.

We are who we are not because of what we do or accomplish.

Our identity comes from being loved and accepted by God. We belong...

And that is enough.

Life with God is easier than we think. Most of us are simply trying too hard. We're straining and we're stressing, but all that effort is for nothing.

God doesn't want your works, He wants you.

Why? Because you belong. You are family, and that's all that matters.

CHAPTER 17 BIG IDEAS

"I was so foolish and ignorant... yet I still belong to You." (Psalm 72.22-23)

Most of us spend years of our lives doing our best to fit it. We're like chameleons, changing our look to blend in with the surroundings.

As much as we try to fit in, we find ourselves still questioning, "Do I really fit here?"

"Fitting in" is always a moving target. It's not a once-and-then-done proposition.

God doesn't want us to spend our lives trying to fit in. Instead, He offers something radically different: the right to belong.

Belonging gives us peace and rest in a way that fitting in never can.

Our identity comes from being loved and accepted by God. We belong and that is enough.

QUESTIONS
FOR INDIVIDUAL &/OR GROUP STUDY

1. Who is a character you tried to play at some point in your life?

2. When you look at old pictures of yourself, what is an obvious change that you can see in yourself today (besides age)?

3. How have you tried to fit in but failed? What happened? How did it make you feel?

4. Do you have a clear sense of belonging in your own family? Why or why not?

5. How does God giving us the right to belong produce peace and rest in our lives?

6. How much of your identity is built on the truth that you are loved and accepted by God—that you belong and that's enough?

He delights to give good gifts to His sons and daughters.
—Trip Lee (For My Good)

For the Lord delights in His people.
(Psalm 149.4 NLT)

18. DELIGHT

The word delight hasn't had much of a place in my vocabulary. Honestly, I use it most when ordering a pizza from Papa Murphy's. It's spelled a little different, deLITE, but it sounds the same. And I'll admit it, I take delight in eating pizza. By the way, have you tried the deLITE Thai Chicken pizza? Absolutely uh-may-zing!

Sometimes I wonder if anyone else thinks about pizza as much as I do. It's embarrassing how often pizza is on my mind. I think about it, dream about it, want it...

And when I finally get some, I delight in it.

Lately, I've become more interested in the word delight and it surprisingly has nothing to do with consuming pizza.

I read a verse from the Psalms in my Bible reading plan one day that just stopped me in my tracks. I saw something that I hadn't noticed before.

Not only was I reading something that caught my attention, but in that moment, I felt as if the Spirit of God was whispering to me too.

I read, "For the Lord delights in His people." (Psalm 149.4 NLT).

As I read the verse, I sensed the whisper of God, "Yes, it's true. I absolutely delight in you."

To be truthful, I'm much more used to that part of religion where we talk about how much we love God and want to do big things for Him...

But I'm not always tuned in to the fact that God absolutely delights in His people, and more specifically, that He delights in me.

Maybe you already know this and sense it in your life on a daily basis.

For me, this was a refreshing revelation.

TOBACCO AND SUGAR

When I was younger, my parents were friends with an elderly British couple, Reggie and Ellen, who lived in our neighborhood and attended our church. They were characters. They came from a different era and culture and had the coolest accents.

Sometimes, when Ellen was over at our house, she'd fall asleep while sitting on the couch and her false teeth would slip out and land on her chest. It was both hilarious and disturbing all at the same time. Reggie had a little metal box contraption that he used to roll his own cigarettes, and I loved to watch him do it. Reggie and Ellen were fascinating people.

This quirky elderly couple delighted in children. They adored us, not because we did anything special or noteworthy, and not because we looked or sounded anything like them, but just because we were kids. They delighted in us, just because.

There are two things I remember about Reggie and the church we attended together:

1) He would be standing on the steps of the entrance of the church, rolling his own cigarette and smoking it right before

the service started each Sunday morning. Even back then, smoking was pretty much looked down upon by the church, but Reggie was 80-some years old and had started his habit when smoking was considered healthy. Nobody was going to tell Reggie he couldn't smoke at church.

2) He always brought large bags of candy with him to distribute to all the kids after church. We all gathered around him the moment the church service ended. To each child, he would smile, say something kind, give a little side-hug, and then give some candy. I guess what I remember about Reggie and church boils down to tobacco and sugar.

Of course, we loved Reggie and looked forward to seeing him at church each week. We came to depend on that weekly dose of sugar from him. But I'm certain Reggie enjoyed the whole thing even more than we did. In the most pure and wonderful way, he delighted in us kids, just because.

In a way, Reggie reminds me of God.

God delights in me too.

Like, He gets a kick out of just watching me! He beams with pride like the parent of a toddler who is taking his first steps. He is impressed with my amateurish artwork; He puts it up for display on Heaven's refrigerator.

He has a picture of me in His wallet.

He smiles when I'm sleeping (you know, all sweaty and puffy-lipped, able to sleep through anything).

He delights in me, not in what I've accomplished or achieved, but just because I exist. I am His child, His beloved.

LEARNING HOW TO BE-LOVED

Most of us are familiar with what the Father said concerning Jesus...

"This is My beloved Son, in whom I am well pleased." (Matthew 3.17 NKJV)

We have no struggle believing that the Father delighted in His Son.

But what we often fail to see is that we too are His beloved, and He is well pleased with us.

Just like I don't tend to use the word "delight" very often, I can't even think of a time in conversation when I have used the word "beloved." Perhaps it's because it seems like an old-timey word, like maybe something from a Shakespeare play.

Beloved means to be dearly loved, to be dear to the heart.

We are God's kids, His sons and daughters, and we are dearly loved by Him. We are dear to His heart. He delights in us. We are beloved. And He is well pleased with us.

I want to use a little wordplay here:

As the beloved of God we need to learn how to be-loved.

We need to finally come to terms with the fact that He always has and always will delight in us. When we're good, bad, weak, strong, secure, insecure, full of faith, fearful, helping others, causing harm, being studious, being absolutely silly...

Regardless, we need to get it in our heads: God delights in us.

CHAPTER 18 BIG IDEAS

"For the Lord delights in His people." (Psalm 149.4 NLT)

Reading that verse, I sensed the whisper of God, "Yes, it's true. I absolutely delight in you."

I'm much more used to that part of religion where we talk about how much we love God and want to do big things for Him...

But I'm not always tuned in to the fact that God absolutely delights in His people, and more specifically, that He delights in me.

We have no struggle believing that the Father delighted in His Son.

But what we often fail to see is that we too are His beloved, and He is well pleased with us.

As the beloved of God we need to learn how to be-loved.

We need to finally come to terms with the fact that He always has and always will delight in us. When we're good, bad, weak, strong, secure, insecure, full of faith, fearful, helping others, causing harm, being studious, being absolutely silly...

We need to get it in our heads: God delights in us.

QUESTIONS
FOR INDIVIDUAL &/OR GROUP STUDY

1. What are some old-timey words that you don't feel comfortable using in conversation?

2. What is something you delight in? Why?

3. Do you tend to be more comfortable focusing on all the big things you will do for God or focusing on how much He delights in you?

4. Why is it challenging to believe we are God's beloved, and He is well pleased with us?

5. What are some ways we can learn to be-loved by God?

6. What does knowing that God delights in you change in your life?

Her hair reminds me of a warm safe place, where as a child I'd hide, and pray for the thunder and the rain to quietly pass me by.
—Axl Rose (Sweet Child O' Mine)

And we're caught within the crossfire of Heaven and Hell, and we're searching for shelter...
—Brandon Flowers (Crossfire)

The name of the Lord is a strong tower; the righteous run to it and are safe.
(Proverbs 18.10)

19. SAFE

Looking back on my childhood years, I'm pretty sure the mission statement of the church I grew up in must have been something like, "We exist to scare the hell out of everyone." And while I can't speak for how it worked on everyone else, I do know they were doing an excellent job of it with me.

It was the late 70's and early 80's, and the church was pretty obsessed with the rapture. They showed end-times films, like "A Thief in the Night," which featured a cover of Larry Norman's 1969 song "I Wish We'd All Been Ready."

The goal of these kinds of movies? Scare you out of the grip of hell and into the Kingdom of God. The problem, for me anyway, was that being scared was the ongoing by-product. I was permanently scared.

The lyrics to "I Wish We'd All Been Ready" haunted me.

"Life was filled with guns and war, and everyone got trampled on the floor. I wish we'd all been ready.

Children died, the days grew cold. A piece of bread could buy a bag of gold. I wish we'd all been ready.

There's no time to change your mind, the Son has come, and you've been left behind."

Programmed in my mind after hearing that song were the words, "Children died... There's no time... You've been left behind."

This is a heavy weight for a kid to carry around. Not exactly something that produces peace or rest, but it definitely inspired a whole bunch of strain and stress.

TAKING SHOTS AT THE WOUNDED

Yes, I had nightmares about missing the rapture, watching heads being chopped off in the guillotine, accidentally getting the mark of the beast, and a variety of other apocalyptic terrors.

And there were a number of times when, coming home from school and finding no evidence of family members, I'd panic and assume the worst: I had missed the rapture. For the next few minutes (until my mom came back from visiting with a friend), I'd frantically devise my ridiculous escape and survival plan. My plans always included a good supply of beef jerky, Skittles, and pepperoni sticks in my backpack.

Then there was the guest evangelist who came and preached at our church about the evils of Christian pop star Amy Grant and all other Christian rock music that would certainly send us straight to hell. He had me convinced there was going to be no place at Heaven's table reserved with my name on it.

During this time, I wasn't exactly feeling safe in the church, in the Kingdom of God, or with God—not because of anything God was saying to me, but because of all the other messages and images people used to communicate for Him.

It kind of reminds me of the one time I went paintballing with a group of friends. We got our equipment and were given all the instructions about how to play. When you've been hit, you're supposed to hold your gun over your head and yell, "Hit!" repeatedly as you walk off the field of play.

That way you're supposed to be safe and no one will take shots at you.

Except they do. That's what happened to me anyway. Walking off the field, holding my gun high above my head, yelling "Hit! I'm Hit. Don't hit me 'cause I've already been hit!" And do you know what those suckers did? They shot me. Even people from my own team took shots at me. I got pelted with paintballs when I was supposed to be safe. That was the first time and the last time I played paintball.

This happens in church too. I've always expected the church to be a safe place, except it isn't always safe. People take shots at the wounded all the time.

A PLACE AT THE TABLE

When I was 9 years old, my grandparents got into an argument with my parents. They were upset about how my parents disciplined me and my siblings. The discipline in question? No dessert after dinner.

Seeing how sugar motivated me, this method of discipline seemed perfectly reasonable in my estimation. Sugar often kept me in good form and on my best behavior. The truth is, sugar still motivates me. It's the number one reason I go to the gym. I work out for sugar credits.

Well, my grandparents blew up and told our family to leave. And that was it. Even after multiple attempts by my dad to smooth things over, my grandparents—his parents—wanted nothing to do with him or us. No more family dinners. No more birthday gifts. No more Christmas together. I didn't see or hear from them again. My place at their table was gone, forever.

You can see how I've acquired a certain level of anxiety about my place at the table.

The impression I got from church was, "If you mess up, you will most likely no longer have a place at the table. God, the angry judge, will lay down the law and tell you to leave. And that will be it."

I'm so thankful for a much more generous view of the family of God that I have today. I'm no longer having nightmares about heads rolling and accidentally taking the mark of the beast.

I am secure, confident, assured that my place at the table is saved and it is safe.

THERE ISN'T A SAFER PLACE TO BE

Perhaps the most vivid expression of the Gospel in story-form is the parable of the Prodigal Son. In this story, we see a loving Father who isn't removing places at the table because of the sins and failings of his children, but rather, he is saving them and keeping them safe.

The Father's house is a safe place for prodigals.

The Father's house is safe for me and it is safe for you.

"He has brought you into His own presence, and you are holy and blameless as you stand before Him without a single fault. You must continue to believe this truth and stand firmly in it. Don't drift away from the assurance you received when you heard the Good News." (Colossians 1.22, 23 NLT)

This verse warns us not to drift from the ASSURANCE we have received.

What assurance are we supposed to stick with?

That we've been brought into His presence—that we're holy and blameless as we stand before Him without a single fault. That we have a place at the table, and this is not our doing. It's all Him. The blood of Jesus made, makes, and will continue to make us holy.

This assurance causes us to be secure and confident, knowing that our place at the table is saved and it is safe.

The Kingdom of God is a safe place.

We are safe, and at home, with God.

In fact, there isn't a safer place to be! God doesn't want us to live in a constant state of anxiety and fear over our relationship with Him, questioning, "Are we in or are we out, are we out of time, have we been left behind?"

Instead, He wants us to be safe and secure in Him.

"You've always given me breathing room, a place to get away from it all, a lifetime pass to Your safe-house, an open invitation as Your guest. You've always taken me seriously, God, made me welcome among those who know and love You." (Psalm 61.3-5 MSG)

CHAPTER 19 BIG IDEAS

"The name of the Lord is a strong tower; the righteous run to it and are safe." (Proverbs 18.10)

The impression I got from church was, "If you mess up, you will most likely no longer have a place at the table. God, the angry judge, will lay down the law and tell you to leave. And that will be it."

I'm so thankful for a much more generous view of the family of God that I have today. I am secure, confident, assured that my place at the table is saved and it is safe.

The Father's house is a safe place for prodigals.

The Father's house is safe for me and it is safe for you.

The Kingdom of God is a safe place.

We are safe, and at home, with God.

There isn't a safer place to be! God doesn't want us to live in a constant state of anxiety and fear over our relationship with Him, questioning, "Are we in or are we out, are we out of time, have we been left behind?"

Instead, He wants us to be safe and secure in Him.

QUESTIONS
FOR INDIVIDUAL &/OR GROUP STUDY

1. Describe a time when you did not feel safe.

2. When have you felt like you had a secure place at the table?

3. How is the Father's house a safe place for prodigals?

4. What are some messages others have given "for" God that gave you the impression the Kingdom of God is not a safe place?

5. How have you grown in your confidence with God?

6. How can we help others to feel safe and secure in their relationship with God?

Kindness in your eyes, I guess you heard me cry.
You smiled at me, like Jesus to a child.
—George Michael (Jesus to a Child)

His kindness lasts for a lifetime.
(Psalm 30.5 NCV)

20. KINDNESS

My favorite teacher from all my years of school was my high school art teacher, Mr. Kirstein. The reason? He was kind to me.

His kindness made me feel like the art class was a safe place. I looked forward to being there. As a result, I learned and grew in confidence. I excelled in art, not because of huge reservoirs of natural talent, but because of a kind teacher.

Recently, I came to the conclusion that kindness is a simple, user-friendly, and easy-to-understand way of describing grace.

Even a child can understand the concept of kindness.

And although I love studying, thinking, and talking about grace (it is absolutely my favorite Kingdom of God subject), I've found that some people can't go with you when you're talking about grace because they think of it as some abstract or complex theological subject.

When we say something about "The grace of God..." not everyone is sure what this means, but when we say something about "The kindness of God..." it is straight forward and self-explanatory.

God is kind.

He is kind to you and He is kind to me.

It is His nature to be kind. His kindness is dependable and trustworthy.

In His kindness, God saved us. And His kindness doesn't stop there!

"If God didn't hesitate to put everything on the line for us, embracing our condition and exposing Himself to the worst by sending His own Son, is there anything else He wouldn't gladly and freely do for us?" (Romans 8.32 MSG)

PARTICIPANTS

The incredible kindness of God is constant. He delights in us. He gives good gifts to His children.

"Every good and perfect gift is from above, coming down from the Father... who does not change like shifting shadows." (James 1.17 NIV)

And as recipients of this kindness, we also become participants in it.

How does God show His kindness to us? Often times it is through people, His people.

The Bible says we are the body of Christ...

"You are Christ's body—that's who you are! You must never forget this." (1 Corinthians 12.27 MSG)

We are His hands and feet.

We are the hands that prepare a meal for the hungry and the hurting.

We are the feet that go to the store to purchase school supplies for underprivileged children.

We are the arms that hug and console.

We are the mouths that speak blessings and words of encouragement.

We are agents of His kindness in the world, tangible expressions of His grace to all of His children (those who are close and those who are far away, sons and daughters who are at home, and the prodigals who have wandered away).

Because we are recipients of God's kindness, we willingly participate in God's plan to show kindness to those who do not know Him yet.

Because God delights in us, we are able to delight in others.

We put judgment on the shelf (we let God deal with that).

We are 100% present, in the moment, delighting in people...

Giving grace, showing kindness.

SAFE TO BE AROUND, SAFE TO BE WITH

You know something interesting about the grace of God?

It could easily be described as irresponsible and not a wise investment.

A risk management expert would disapprove.

"Too risky. Costs too much. Not enough guarantees."

But God didn't ask a risk management expert for approval before pouring out His grace and kindness on humanity. He's not worried about being taken advantage of because He already decided to give what isn't deserved...

And that's what grace is. Underserved, unearned favor. Kindness, just because.

No strings attached. Nothing reciprocal expected. This is not an exchange of one thing for another. No demands are given with the gift.

Kindness, just because.

When we experience this type of kindness, we realize something about the person who is giving it...

They are safe to be around, safe to be with.

I don't have to hide or pretend that I'm somebody else.

I can be me, because I am who they showed kindness to— not me playing the part of someone else, not me in disguise, not me lying about my resume. Just me.

As the hands and feet of Jesus in the world, we need to be agents of His grace. We must show the kindness of God to all His children, everywhere.

And when we participate in showing kindness, we send a clear message to the world that says...

"We are safe. We're safe to be around, safe to be with. You can be you—no hiding, no pretending, no worries, no judgment. Our agenda is simple and pure: to be kind. We expect nothing in return. No demands are given with this gift."

It's cool to see how kindness tears down walls that separate us.

When our church puts on the annual "Great Big Backpack Give" each year for underprivileged children in our community, my wife and I get more hugs from complete strangers...

Thanking us, genuinely moved, full of gratitude.

Kindness does that. It brings people together. It tears down walls. It sends a clear message to the world that says, "We are safe."

SANCTUARY

I think churches should be safe places.

There's an old word for that: sanctuary. It means "refuge, shelter, a safe place." I want people to know that our church is a safe place to go, regardless of what's going on in their lives.

Not too long ago, someone from our church came by unexpectedly during the week. She seemed a little embarrassed and had tears in her eyes as she said to me, "I don't know why I'm here. It's just that I'm expecting a phone call from my ex-husband about our custody plan, and I don't think it will go well. I guess I wanted to be somewhere safe, somewhere that feels like family when I get the call."

She was looking for sanctuary, a safe place—exactly what the church should be.

It's important to point out that the church isn't a structure or building. We're not talking about physical places of shelter...

We're talking about relationship, people providing safety and sanctuary for others. The church is people—it's us, which means we need to be safe people, sanctuary people.

I remember this old song we used to sing in the church called "Blessed Be The Name Of The Lord" (it was one of those songs that had "motions" to accompany it). Part of the song quotes Proverbs 18.10, "The name of the Lord is a strong tower, the righteous run into it, and they are saved."

This song, and verse of the Bible, reminds us that God's name and reputation is connected to refuge, sanctuary, a place of strength and safety.

As God's Kingdom people, I hope we are building a reputation as being out-of-this-world kind and safe.

I WANT TO SHOW GOD'S KINDNESS TO HIM

There's a fascinating story in the Old Testament about King David. At some point during his reign, he asks the question, "Is there anyone to whom I can show kindness for Jonathan's sake?" (2 Samuel 9.1 NLT)

Jonathan was David's friend and the previous king's son. Jonathan had died in battle some time ago. David wondered whether there were any other family members of Jonathan's that he could show kindness to, for the sake of his friend.

I like the question he asks his advisors, "Is there anyone to whom I can show kindness for Jonathan's sake?"

I think we should be inquiring, like David, "Is there anyone to whom I can show kindness? There must be someone…"

David continued to press the issue. He said, "I want to show God's kindness to them." (2 Samuel 9.3 NLT)

The answer David received from his advisors was "YES." Yes, there is someone, and his name is Mephibosheth. He is crippled and poor. David welcomed Mephibosheth into his home, as family, and gave him a place at the table. He showed God's kindness to Mephibosheth.

And you know what? If we ask that same question, the answer will always be YES. Yes, there is someone.

Something fascinating to me about this story of David & Mephibosheth is how David said, "I want to show God's kindness to him."

My kindness is mediocre at best. But God's kindness…

Well, it's the best.

Let's show God's kindness to a world that so desperately needs it.

Check out the appendix for a collection of kindness Tweets and Scriptures.

CHAPTER 20 BIG IDEAS

"His kindness lasts for a lifetime." (Psalm 30.5 NCV)

Kindness is a simple, user-friendly, and easy-to-understand way of describing grace.

The incredible kindness of God is constant. He delights in us. He gives good gifts to His children.

And as recipients of this kindness, we also become participants in it.

God often shows His kindness through people, His people. "You are Christ's body—that's who you are! You must never forget this." (1 Corinthians 12.27 MSG)

We are His hands and feet.

Because we are recipients of God's kindness, we willingly participate in God's plan to show kindness to those who do not know Him yet.

Because God delights in us, we are able to delight in others.

We put judgment on the shelf (we'll let God deal with that).

We are 100% present, in the moment, delighting in people...

Giving grace, showing kindness.

When we participate in showing kindness, we send a clear message to the world that says...

"We are safe. We're safe to be around, safe to be with. You can be you—no hiding, no pretending, no worries, no judgment. Our agenda is simple and pure: to be kind. We expect nothing in return. No demands are given with this gift."

Kindness tears down walls that separate us.

QUESTIONS
FOR INDIVIDUAL &/OR GROUP STUDY

1. Who has been especially kind to you? How did they show kindness to you?

2. How is God kind to us?

3. How has God been kind to you through other people?

4. What holds us back from truly delighting in others?

5. Are you safe—safe to be around, safe to be with? How do people know?

6. True kindness expects nothing in return. Why is it so difficult for us to give with no strings attached?

Everything is right with you, after all that I've been through.
—Macy Gray (Time Of My Life)

They will name Him Immanuel, which means "God is with us."
(Matthew 1.23 NCV)

21. WITH

When my mom was first in the hospital without any clear diagnosis, it was December, right before Christmas time. In our family, Christmas is kind of a big deal—and at least part of it is always celebrated at my parents' house.

We were all hoping and praying for my mom's healing. The Christmas miracle we wanted was for my mom to be well and at home, celebrating with the family for the holidays.

Unfortunately, it soon became evident we would need to make other plans for Christmas. My mom wouldn't be coming home, not for Christmas anyway, and we would need to break from the usual family tradition.

It kind of took the wind out of my sails. This would be the first time in my life that we wouldn't be celebrating Christmas at my parents' house. I'm Mr. Modern about most everything in life, but when it comes to Christmas, I don't want anyone messing with my tradition!

We made plans to celebrate Christmas dinner together as a family in the hospital. The hospital was gracious and gave us a conference room to use.

I cooked the entire dinner at home and packed everything in plastic containers to take to the hospital. We put a fake

Christmas tree and some decorations in the car and headed out.

The whole family was there at the hospital. It wasn't the ideal location for celebrating Christmas, but it was our only choice.

Sure, we would have rather been at my parents' house. Honestly, I would have rather been eating my mom's cooking. But none of that mattered. There was something bigger at stake...

We were getting to spend Christmas WITH my mom. The traditions and locations weren't nearly as important as being WITH her.

We ate Christmas dinner on paper plates (and the food was reheated in a hospital microwave). We sat in conference room chairs around a plastic Christmas tree opening presents. And my mom was there, in a hospital gown, attached to an IV, not feeling good at all...

But completely satisfied that her family was all there WITH her on Christmas.

As far as Christmases go, this was certainly one of the most memorable, and it will always remind me of the significance of experiencing life together WITH the ones we love.

We need to be reminded from time to time that life WITH God is the big deal.

The traditions and locations are not the main thing. Life WITH God is.

Life WITH God, regardless of the circumstances and storms we might be facing, fills us with peace and rest.

HUSTLE AND PEACE AND REST

It seems ironic that my "word of the year" (a word I chose to represent my focus, expecting that it would accurately represent the trajectory of my life over the course of this year) is "hustle."

Just to clarify, my use of the word hustle has to do with getting up early, working hard, being quick on my feet, having some street smarts, and getting stuff done, NOT doing illegal things to make money.

Still, my theme for the year seems ironic.

Here I am, writing a book about how God wants to give us peace and rest, and my word of the year is hustle. These words seem like they might be at odds with each other.

Someone could ask, "Do you want peace and rest or do you want to hustle?" Which is it going to be?

The thing is, I'm not a real big "either/or" kind of guy. I tend to be a fan of "both/and..."

I carved out a month for myself this year to write a book. If you're going to write a book in a month, let's just say you kind of have to hustle. But I also took a break from doing everything else. I'm pausing, having a Selah moment, enjoying some peace and rest while I hustle and write. For me, trying to do everything I normally do AND write a book on top of it all would be a whole lot of strain and stress.

So I chose to hustle and get some peace and rest.

Receiving God's peace and rest doesn't mean a life of inactivity. It doesn't mean we just nap all day, listen to Bob Marley, and stop being productive.

I'm not writing "The Lazy Christian Manifesto" here.

Receiving God's peace and rest does mean we've come to terms with the fact that we're not the heroes of our own stories. We are fully aware that there is only room for one Hero in our lives.

And it does mean we've said "no thanks" to the world's way of strain and stress.

It also means that we're not nearly as focused on doing what we do in life FOR God, but we are completely excited about this life that we have WITH God.

ADVENTURE

"This resurrection life you received from God is not a timid, grave-tending life. It's adventurously expectant, greeting God with a childlike 'What's next, Papa?' God's Spirit touches our spirits and confirms who we really are. We know who He is, and we know who we are: Father and children. And we know we are going to get what's coming to us—an unbelievable inheritance! We go through exactly what Christ goes through. If we go through the hard times with Him, then we're certainly going to go through the good times with Him!" (Romans 8:15-17 MSG)

The Kingdom life isn't a timid, weak, unproductive, apathetic, boring one.

Nope. It's adventurously expectant. It's life WITH God!

We're asking Him, "What are we going to do today Daddy?"

In the good times and the bad times, one thing is constant: we have life WITH God.

Life WITH God isn't static, it's not a stand-still or a power outage, and it doesn't prevent us from having amazing adventures, creating beautiful masterpieces, or making a major difference in the world.

Life WITH God is active, vibrant, and alive. It's having the Creator of the universe guiding, leading, revealing, speaking...

And we are fully present, 100% WITH Him.

Aware. Taking notice. Attentive. Listening, even to His whisper.

Life with God is about receiving. We receive His love. We receive His kindness, His grace. We receive His acceptance. We receive His peace. We receive His rest.

We receive His invitation to adventure WITH Him.

This is so much bigger than traditions and locations. This is life WITH God!

"In Him we live and move and exist. It is as some of your poets have said, 'We too are His children.'" (Acts 17.28 GNT)

SHOULD HAVE BEEN FIRED

For those who primarily see their relationship with God as being all about what they will do FOR God, the pressure is on…

Everything will be measured by what they have accomplished.

They become the hero or villain of their story based on their own success or failure.

There's no time to sleep, no time for rest, and there is very little peace.

It is the way of strain and stress.

And it's not at all what God has in mind for us.

Remember what Jesus said?

"Are you tired? Worn out? Burned out on religion? Come to me. Get away with me and you'll recover your life. I'll show you how to take a real rest. Walk with me and work with me—watch how I do it. Learn the unforced rhythms of grace. I won't lay anything heavy or ill-fitting on you. Keep company with me and you'll learn to live freely and lightly." (Matthew 11.28-30 MSG)

Come to me.

Get away WITH me. I'll show you how…

Walk WITH me and work WITH me; watch how I do it.

Learn the unforced rhythms of grace.

Keep company WITH me and you'll learn how to live freely and lightly.

Jesus is describing life WITH God, not just life FOR God.

By the way, did you know the disciples weren't Jesus' employees?

That's right. They weren't working FOR Jesus, they were experiencing life together WITH Him. They were His friends. They ate together, went on adventures together, laughed together, argued together, relaxed together, did big things together, they even went on vacation together.

The disciples experienced and enjoyed life WITH Jesus.

If they had been employees, most, if not all of them, should have been fired.

And it still blows me away that Jesus kept Judas as a friend all the way to the cross.

It doesn't seem right—like a one-way relationship. Jesus kept him as a friend, while Judas was scheming, stealing, sneaking around, and selling Him out. But Jesus didn't cut Judas off. He took that friendship all the way to the cross.

You know what? He has done the same thing for us too.

He hasn't cut us off. Even when it's been a one-way relationship, Jesus kept us as friends—all the way to the cross.

All our scheming, stealing, sneaking around, and selling-out didn't keep us from God's love.

If we were employees, we would have been fired by now.

But we're not employees.

We are family. We are friends.

We have life WITH God, and this means loads of adventure, and an ongoing supply of Kingdom peace and rest. This is the life!

CARPET STAINS

I've had plenty of bosses, co-workers, teachers, classmates, neighbors, and church friends over the years, and I'm not currently experiencing life together WITH them. Why?

Because the nature of our relationship was always just about the job, the class, the project, the church...

And when we no longer worked at the same job, attended the same school, lived in the same neighborhood, or went to the same church—we were no longer friends.

I know that sounds harsh, but it's the reality.

Of course we'd be kind if we happened to run into each other at the mall or a sporting event, but we're not really friends—we're acquaintances. We know about each other and we have some history together, but we don't really know each other. We think kindly of each other, but we aren't experiencing life WITH each other.

I like them and they like me, but neither one of us is going to do anything to keep the relationship going. We're in different places now, and know we're not going to be experiencing life together.

There are other friends, for whom the same set of circumstances are true. We no longer work together, go to the same church, attend classes together, or live in the same neighborhood, but we are still experiencing life WITH each other.

We spend time together. We talk. We vacation together. We exchange gifts. We celebrate with each other and we comfort each other. These aren't just Facebook friends, these are friends we continue to share life WITH.

What's the difference? Why do we carry on in relationship with some people, and move on from others when circumstances change in our lives creating a physical distance between us?

Here's what I've learned from experience: the relationships that go beyond time together at the job, in the neighborhood, at a class, or being at the same church are the ones that survive.

These are the people who have been in my home, and I have been in their homes.

We once had some good friends over for dinner. Although we used to live near each other and attend the same church, we now live in different cities and attend different churches, but our friendship continued beyond that.

Sitting around the dining room table, we were enjoying a meal together. Our conversation was suddenly interrupted by an unusual sound...

Their toddler, sitting in a highchair at the table, was making that disturbing pre-throw-up heaving noise. He was milliseconds away from exploding.

I will never forget what happened next. My wife lunged with her hands cupped and caught, mid-air, about 2/3 of the vomit! I was stunned. Who does that?!!?! And why?

I personally always run away from vomit, and never towards it. I can sort of understand why someone might move toward their own child who is vomiting, but not somebody else's kid. I don't care what kind of carpet is at risk.

Everyone scurried to clean things up in the dining room.

Later, when I asked my wife why she did it, she said, "I don't really know. I think subconsciously I was concerned about the carpet, but there wasn't time to think. It was just a reaction."

These are the kinds of things that happen when friends are in the homes of friends...

I'm sure you have your stories too.

Carpets get stained. Memories are made. Life is shared together WITH them.

UNPAINTED MOMENTS

Did you know Jesus offered hospitality and had the disciples in His home?

They asked Him "Where do you live?" (John 1.38 GNT)

He invited them to come and see. "So they went with Him and saw where He lived, and spent the rest of that day with Him." (John 1.39 GNT)

I love this.

It's a tiny little detail in Scripture, but its significance is huge to me. Jesus had a place (whether owned, rented, borrowed, or whatever). Not only did Jesus have a place, but He invited His friends over too.

I can totally picture Jesus barbequing for them in His backyard. You better believe they sat around in His family room having some fantastic pita chips and hummus. I imagine one of His friends spilled wine on the carpet or couch, leaving a permanent stain behind (probably Judas).

We know about ministry trips the disciples had with Jesus, but I think we need to be reminded that they also spent time together in their homes, eating and laughing and relaxing. Life together, WITH each other. I wish religious art reflected this—the eating, the laughing, the relaxing—at least once in a while. The paintings we have do a great job of showing the more serious moments, but I think there's value in the less-than-serious moments of life too.

Perhaps the real roots of our relationships are actually forged in the "unpainted, un-photogenic, and un-art-worthy" moments of life together.

The friends I have that continued beyond our shared jobs are more than co-workers. We've been experiencing life together, WITH each other. The relationship we share is about more than a shared job or neighborhood...

It's about life together.

And this is exactly what God has in mind for us: life together WITH Him.

Not just doing big things FOR Him, but life together WITH Him.

Not always photogenic and glamorous, but WITH Him...

Yes, even while eating, laughing, and relaxing.

WHISPERS

Life WITH God is easier than we think. Most of us are simply trying too hard. We're straining and we're stressing, but all that effort is for nothing.

God doesn't want your works, He wants you.

And there's more.

The life that He has for you includes peace and rest.

Sounds too easy, doesn't it? Just too good to be true.

Exactly.

Too good to be true is God's specialty.

Unmerited. Undeserved. Unexpected.

The impossible.

That's His way.

He is the true Hero of the story—the Hero who saves the day, settles the score, makes a way where there seems to be no way...

He loves us more than we know.

He loves us now, today. And not just some future, perfected version of ourselves, but our real selves. He's not disappointed in us. Actually, He delights in us.

I'm pretty sure all the really important things He wants us to know in life, He whispers to us...

And I hope you've heard God whispering to you as you read this book.

CHAPTER 21 BIG IDEAS

They will name Him Immanuel, which means "God is with us." (Matthew 1.23 NCV)

We need to be reminded from time to time that life WITH God is the big deal.

Receiving God's peace and rest does mean we've come to terms with the fact that we're not the heroes of our own stories. We are fully aware that there is only room for one Hero in our lives.

It also means that we're not nearly as focused on doing what we do in life FOR God, but we are completely excited about this life that we have WITH God.

The Kingdom life isn't a timid, weak, unproductive, apathetic, boring one. It's adventurously expectant. It's life WITH God! We're asking Him, "What are we going to do today Daddy?"

In the good times and the bad times, one thing is constant: we have life WITH God.

Life WITH God isn't static, it's not a stand-still or a power outage, and it doesn't prevent us from having amazing adventures, creating beautiful masterpieces, or making a major difference in the world.

Life WITH God is active, vibrant, and alive. It's having the Creator of the universe guiding, leading, revealing, speaking... And we are fully present, 100% WITH Him. Aware. Taking notice. Attentive. Listening, even to His whisper.

We're not employees. We are family. We are friends.

We have life WITH God, and this means loads of adventure, and an ongoing supply of Kingdom peace and rest. This is the life.

Relationships that go beyond time together at the job, in the neighborhood, at a class, or being at the same church are the ones that survive.

These are the people who have been in my home, and I have been in their homes.

It's about life together. Not always photogenic and glamorous, but WITH… Yes, even while eating, laughing, and relaxing.

Life WITH God is easier than we think. Most of us are simply trying too hard. We're straining and we're stressing, but all that effort is for nothing.

God doesn't want your works, He wants you.

And there's more; the life that He has for you includes peace and rest.

QUESTIONS
FOR INDIVIDUAL &/OR GROUP STUDY

1. What's a tradition that is big and has significance in your family?

2. Be honest. If you were God's employee, should you have been fired by now? How does it encourage you to know you're not God's employee?

3. How is life WITH God different than life FOR God?

4. How does peace and rest work with an adventure-filled life WITH God?

5. Real relationships are built in the non-photogenic, non-glamorous moments of life together (even while eating, laughing, and relaxing). In what ways have you seen this to be true in your relationships? How about in your relationship with God?

6. What has God whispered to you as you've read this book?

APPENDIX

Just recently I went on a kindness rant on Twitter, so I thought I'd share some of the Tweets with you...

Kindness is like a shelter from the storm—a safe place where worries fade and courage grows. When we're kind, people recognize that we are safe.

The real measure of kindness isn't really in what you did for someone, it's in how they feel as a result of what you did. Sometimes I claim certain actions as "kind," but nobody felt anything.

David said "I want to show God's kindness to them" (2 Sam. 9.3) Notice – he didn't say "my kindness," he said "God's kindness." That's a whole notha level of kindness.

When we show someone God's kindness... Where does that kindness come from? Whose standard does it meet? Who gets the credit for it?

Micah 6.8
The Lord has told you what is good... to love being kind to others.

When I show someone God's kindness....
I know this – God is more kind than me. He's more patient. He's more understanding. He gives more chances than I do.

I'm not sure if anyone has ever benefited from my rightness, but my kindness can do wonders.

Being right doesn't have the power to soften hearts. Being kind does.

When you're right about something, you're all alone in feeling good about it. When you're kind, you AND everyone else feels good about it.

I do enjoy being right. Don't you? However, it gets all twisted when we have greater satisfaction in being right than we do in being kind.

People complain about someone who "has to be right all the time." Can't remember hearing anyone complain about someone who "is kind all the time"

The one who is right all the time lays a heavy burden on others. The one who is kind refreshes.

Kindness refreshes others. "Your kindness has often refreshed the hearts of God's people." —Philemon 1.7 // Be refreshing. Be kind.

Kindness brings change more than rightness does. "In kindness he takes us firmly by the hand & leads us into radical life-change." —Rom. 2.4

Kindness - why often tone is more important than content - it's easy to be right but be oh so wrong.

Being right can feel good, but so does eating pizza—doesn't mean it's actually good for you. Being kind feels good AND is good for you.

Being right leaves you feeling superior. Being kind leaves someone else feeling lifted.

Kindness isn't about giving gifts for a job well done—it's best seen in the undeserved, unexpected & total surprise.

Don't be afraid of the kinder, gentler you. Honestly, we all like that version of you better anyway.

Kindness sends a message. It says, "We're not enemies or competitors. I'm for you & truly care." The church needs to be sending this message

When U show kindness, ppl are often interested in what U have 2 say. Unfortunately, many Christians like 2 start w/ "I have something 2 say"

We (the church) are generally known more for our positions (we want people to know we're "right") than for our kindness. That's jacked-up.

Kindness isn't hoping to gain something in return. There's no ulterior motive—it's not a bribe. It is content to simply give & be a blessing

Being kind to someone who is kind to you isn't really kindness—that's more of a transaction. Unexpected kindness is the powerful stuff.

Kind doesn't imply weak. Actually, it requires a lot of strength to be kind.

We live in a world obsessed with the advancement of self. Kindness is all about blessing or "advancing" others.

The world isn't going to thank God for our churchy behavior or holy devotion—but when we show kindness, it actually causes people to say "Thank God!"

When someone tells you, "You're too kind," smile & say "thanks," but just know—it's not true. It's an expression. Nobody is too kind.

I don't believe we've even come close to "too kind" territory, & I'm not worried it will ever happen. Kindness doesn't need a safe mode.

Err on the side of kindness (actually, it's not an error at all).

Our default position isn't kindness. We're selfish & mean. Cain killed his brother & "Me 1st" has prevailed ever since. Kindness is work.

Selfishness & kindness come from different kingdoms. Think about that.

Kindness requires us to make our egos shut up & take a back seat.

Kindness is hard work—it's death to self. This is why the world will never have enough kindness & why it needs it from us so desperately.

Let's be honest: American culture is oriented to being kind to self. We do it so well, there's not much left in the tank for others.

When you're full of yourself there's little room left for kindness to others.

You being right doesn't cheer up the place, but kindness does.

If you're not kind, it makes it difficult for others to care about anything you say.

You'd think if the church was full of God's Spirit, it would be full of kindness.

Kindness is timeless—it is always timely.

People don't need a lecture & a glare from you, they need some kindness & a smile.

If our message isn't kind, I don't think it's really the Gospel.

If the church doesn't sound & feel kind, something is very wrong.

It's only when self is kicked off the throne that kindness can really thrive.

What is kindness? Giving someone what you really want for yourself.

Kindness isn't cheap. You've really got to have some substance to you if you're going to be kind to others.

Christianity and kindness (should) go hand in hand.

Every step away from kindness is a step away from the Gospel.

Kindness is like the sun—it breaks through the clouds and rain, warms our faces, and invites us back outside to enjoy the world again.

Did you know that you being kind is evidence of God's Spirit working in you? Yup, it's true... Galatians 5.22

Kind acts start with kind thoughts.

Kindness is a muscle that has to be exercised. A lot of us have kindness-atrophy.

Kindness initiates, it takes the first step. It isn't waiting for an invitation.

Kindness isn't looking for a payoff or reward. It has no agenda, other than kindness.

You should always clothe yourself with kindness — Colossians 3.12

Kindness doesn't put up fences, it builds bridges.

"It is kindness that I want." —Matthew 12.7 // Make God happy, be kind to people.

Kindness shown to the poor is an act of worship. —Proverbs 14.31 GNT // Perhaps kindness is much more spiritual than we thought....

Being kind might be an inconvenience, but it is also very much a way of life for those who choose to follow Jesus.

Remember that "go the 2nd mile" concept? Yeah, it came from Jesus and it was about kindness.

"2nd Mile" in the dictionary: "Kindness beyond the demands of duty." Exactly what Jesus meant.

One simple way to be kind is to listen (and actually hear).

Kindness doesn't carry a sword. It doesn't have a back-up fighting plan. It's not concerned w/ the preservation or protection of self.

Kindness cares more about people than winning arguments or being right.

You must show kindness and mercy to one another. — Zechariah 7.9   // Sounds like kindness & mercy aren't optional, huh?

Selfishness pursues gain at the expense of others. Kindness pursues the good of others at the expense of self.

One simple way to be kind: put another's feelings before your personal pride. Apologize, & own it, even when you don't feel 100% in the wrong.

When we decide a person matters, we are kind to them. I hate what our lack of kindness reveals about our attitude toward others.

When we are unkind to people it shows a lack of love and value. And this is not good.

Kindness isn't into accounting. It's not keeping a balance sheet. It's not waiting for someone to do something first to deserve your kindness.

Kindness isn't a "you scratch my back & I'll scratch your back" deal. Its simple agenda is to show love & be a blessing, no strings attached.

Want to really stand out? Be unusually & unexpectedly kind.

Kindness warms the soul.

Kindness is others-focused & builds relationships. Self-focus destroys relationships.

I doubt the one who really exercises her "kindness muscle" is lonely.

Kindness doesn't diminish people, it recognizes the inherent worth in others & chooses to add value.

One simple way to be kind: say gracious, encouraging, worth-giving, & value-adding things.

If we Christians can't figure out how to be kind, is there really any point to trying to get "deeper" in our understanding of Scripture?

Our kindness, or lack of it, speaks louder than our statements of faith.

Our kindness, or lack of it, reveals what we truly believe about the Gospel.

You can't be kind and throw a stone at the same time.

Kindness suspends judgment & cares for the individual.

And to your service to God add kindness —2 Peter 1.7 // If you do stuff for God, but aren't kind to people, something is all messed up.

Sometimes balance shouldn't be our goal. Don't aim for neutral ground between cruelty and kindness. Instead, just go all lopsided with kindness.

The absence of kindness sends an "I don't care" message.

Kindness is practical, tangible, clear, obvious... it's so simple to understand—even young children get it.

If I were to explain the concept of grace to a child, I would use the word kindness.

Kindness gives someone a place at the table who doesn't appear to belong.

One simple way to be kind is to give or bring someone food when they weren't expecting it & whether they needed it or not.

One simple way to be kind is to celebrate with someone regarding their good news or good fortune.

One simple way to be kind is to share in someone's sorrow, cry with them, listen to their story, & care.

Also, here are a few of my favorite kindness Scriptures:

Psalm 30.5 NCV
His kindness lasts for a lifetime

Proverbs 14.21 GNT
Kindness shown to the poor is an act of worship.

Isaiah 54.8 NCV
I will show you mercy with kindness forever.

Zechariah 7.9 GNT
You must show kindness and mercy to one another.

Matthew 9.13 NCV
Go and learn what this means: "I want kindness more than I want sacrifices."

Matthew 12.7 GNT
It is kindness that I want.

Galatians 5.22 NIV
The fruit of the Spirit is... kindness...

Colossians 3.12 NCV
You should always clothe yourselves with mercy, kindness, humility, gentleness, & patience.

2 Peter 1.7 NCV
And to your service for God add kindness...

ABOUT THE AUTHOR

Brian Dolleman and his wife Shari have been the Lead Pastors of NWLife Church in Renton, WA since 2007. They both grew up in the Seattle area and love the Northwest. They've been married for 20 years, have been in ministry together for 20 years, and have a 13 year old daughter, Ashah. Brian is committed to building a church for the prodigals—a safe place, with a grace-filled "welcome home" message. Brian has been so personally touched by the incredible grace of our loving God, he had "Changed by Grace" tattooed on his arm. Brian Dolleman blogs & podcasts regularly on his website:
www.northwestleader.com

Made in the USA
San Bernardino, CA
06 January 2015